ISBN 978-0-484-17293-6
PIBN 10555556

Brown Alumni Monthly

May 1983, Vol. 83, No. 8

p-

ks

pages 16-51

In this issue

Departments

Cover photograph by John Forasté

CARRYING THE MAIL

'Cavalier tone'

Editor: The entry in Under the Elms (*BAM*, March) entitled "At Long Last, a Student Center" might more aptly have read, "At What Cost a Student Center?" I was dismayed by the cavalier tone taken in the paragraphs which dealt with Production Workshop. There are certain points of information that I would like to clarify.

When the completed report on the proposed student center was first made public, a somewhat more positive response than a "hue and cry" was undertaken. The Ad Hoc Committee for Production Workshop was formed and it quickly sought to formulate an alternative to the plan contained in the report, a report which had already been presented to the Corporation. The plan proposed to exclude Production Workshop from the student center, thereby excluding one of the most vital and long-lived student groups.

The committee proceeded to collect the signatures of over 3,000 undergraduates on a petition which called for Production Workshop to remain in Faunce House as an integral part of the proposed center.

A feeling that some abstract entity called PW would suffer was not what motivated the committee or what prompted those signatures. Rather, it was a feeling that the continued existence of an activity that annually involves some 300 students in productions and 3,000 as audience members was being threatened.

I fervently hope that Production Workshop will continue to prosper in its new location. Its demise would be a shameful loss. I doubt that there is another university in the United States that can boast an entirely student-run theatre that has been in continuous operation for over twenty-two years. I recognize the importance of the potluck suppers which Ms. Cole envisions. However, I can only mourn that a space whose height and breadth were so admirably suited to theatre productions will now be used to house such suppers.

DANIANNE MIZZY '82
New Haven, Conn.

Women's swimming

Editor: My heart started fluttering as I glanced at the cover (*BAM*, March) —women's swimming as a feature article! As a swimmer at Brown in the dark days before Dave Roach turned the team arou I read with awe about each woman's accomplishments and feelings. I particularl appreciate the answers to "why do you spend so much time just swimming back and forth" and hope my old friends will now understand the joys of water. I'm bursting with pride that women's swimn at Brown is truly a varsity sport and onl wish that I had been there to savor the team's triumph over Princeton. Hearty well-earned congrats to Coach Roach an his team.

CARLA GREENBAUM '78, '81 M.D.
Seattle, Wash.

Editor: Your article on the Brown wo men's swim team was excellent and read it made me proud to be affiliated with th However, I am compelled to ask you to rect your error regarding my occupation. do not work at a "local mental rehabilitat center." I am currently Clinical Assistant Professor in Psychiatry with the Brown U versity Medical School and hold joint appointments at Rhode Island Hospital in t Departments of Rehabilitation Medicine Psychiatry. Please correct this error.

FRANK R. SPARADEO, Ph.D.
Providence

Common sense?

Editor: On a recent visit to Brown, I greeted by hundreds of posters in variou colors, announcing the birth of a conser tive journal named *Common Sense*. I put "conservative" in quotes, because if the posters are any indication, the journal w be more fascist than conservative. The p ers proudly trumpeted plans to "smash liberal monopoly at Brown." What are t planning to do—smash in the skulls of l erals with baseball bats?

Even more disconcerting was the po ers' boastful announcement that *Commo Sense* is generously funded by a conserv foundation. I find it quite frightening to think that right wing organizations are u ing the huge amounts of money they ha at their disposal to alter the political bal at Brown. Normally, I'd be totally in su port of conservative students expressing their views, but not if the students are merely paid mouthpieces for the Moral jority, the John Birch Society, or some o bunch of right wing fanatics.

Unfortunately, there's every reason

There's still time to enroll in Brown's Summer Alumni College June 26-July 2, on the campus

In the mornings you'll be caught up in lectures and discussions with Brown faculty in "A View of the West: 1900-1930, Literature and Society in a Time of Crises."

In the afternoons you'll be immersed in workshops in computers, economics, photography, physical fitness, or stress management.

For more information, call 401 863-2785 or write Summer Alumni College, Box 1920 Brown University, Providence, RI 02912

A program in Brown University's Continuing College

Let your advertising benefit from all four characteristics of Ivy League Group Readers

- **Education**
- **Affluence**
- **Influence**
- **Loyalty** — to their college and its magazine

Send for the 1981 Subscriber Study done by Harvard Business School. It confirms all these characteristics and supports our claim that the Ivy Group is an ideal medium for *selling quality products and places to 403,000 quality people*

The Mortimer Berkowitz Company, Inc.

145 East 63rd St., New York, NY 10021 (212) 753-9740

BROWN ALUMNI MONTHLY · COLUMBIA MAGAZINE · CORNELL ALUMNI NEWS · DARTMOUTH ALUMNI MAGAZINE · HARVARD BUSINESS SCHOOL BULLETIN · THE PENNSYLVANIA GAZETTE · PRINCETON ALUMNI WEEKLY · YALE ALUMNI MAGAZINE and JOURNAL

Ivy League

Vacation Planning Guide

We think we can be of assistance to you in planning your next vacation. Listed below are advertisers offering free booklets or brochures. All you need do to receive this material is circle the corresponding numbers on the coupon and return it to us. We'll do the rest!

1. *THE BIRCHES*—only a special few may experience our 19th Century coastal Maine estate on Blue Hill Harbor. Delight in superb cuisine in an informal and graceful atmosphere. We offer sailing, golfing, tennis, or a daily trip on our own lobster boat. Circle No. 1.

2. *CHINA SIGHTSEEING*—20 itineraries; more than 100 departures to CHINA. For a two-week cultural tour to five Chinese cities, all-inclusive land and air fare from San Francisco is only $2,181. Circle No. 2.

3. *DUNCASTER*—a non-profit retirement community on 72 acres just west of Hartford, CT. Independent living for New England lovers in a congenial and stimulating environment. Sound medical care and other services available for the rest of your life. Circle No. 3.

4. *HORIZON*—start in Paris, then cruise the beautiful French canals on a hotel-boat. Enjoy superb French cuisine. Visit picturesque villages and chateaux. Relax on sundeck or cycle alongside while floating thru Burgundy. Circle No. 4.

5. *LYNN JACHNEY CHARTERS*—private crewed yacht charters in the Caribbean, New England, and the Mediterranean. Virgin Island bareboat listing also available. Personalized service for the perfect sailing vacation for you and your party. Circle No. 5.

6. *JACQUELINE MOSS MUSEUM TOURS*—special art, architecture and archeology tour of CHINA, Oct. 18-Nov. 11. Hong Kong, Hangchow, Shanghai, Kaifeng, Luoyang, Xian, Taiyuan, Datong, Peking. Visit fabulous Ming tombs, Neolithic villages, The Great Wall, imperial palaces, museums. See colossal Buddhas, the army of lifesize terra cotta warriors, magnificent bronzes and ceramics. Expert guiding, limited size group. Circle No. 6.

Ivy League Alumni Magazines
626 Thurston Avenue
Ithaca, NY 14850

B5/83

Please send the vacation/travel information corresponding to the numbers I have circled:

1 2 3 4 5 6

Name *(please print)* ____________________

Address ____________________

City__________ State________ Zip_______

Brown Medical Program; and Dr. Nane
Wenger of Emory University, with who
have had correspondence about womer
cardiacs, is the parent of a Brown class
1982 graduate.

Secondly, in the last paragraph of tl
article there is an unfortunate inversion
the ratio of female to male heart attack
tality. The ratio is 3:1 males to females;
the sentence should read "women have
heart attacks at the rate of 1:3 to men. .

I thank you again for your interest.

LOIS A. MONTEIRO '58 A.B., '70 P
Campus

Author's query

Editor: I'm currently writing *The Wc Woman's Guide to Pregnancy* (to be publi
by a major trade house), and I hope th
BAM will print this letter. I'd like to int
view Brown/Pembroke alumnae and wi
of alumni (and their friends) who have
perienced or are currently having "worl
pregnancies" and are willing to share tl
problems, frustrations, victories, and ac
(both practical and profound). Since th
book is aimed at real women (as oppos
the Super variety), I'd like to talk with
ple whose jobs are lucrative or low-pay
demanding or "cushy," and with wom
who returned to the office after two we
or decided to spend a few years at hor
Naturally, I'll use pseudonyms in the b
when requested.

:all me collect at (914) 941-4386, or drop line at 14 Pocantico Rd., Ossining, 10562.
EAN GRASSO FITZPATRICK '76
A.B., A.M.)
)ssining, N.Y.

ode Brown plates

:ditor: I am writing in reference to some 'n University plates which were pro- d sometime in the early '30s by Spode. were sold by Providence's Tilden ber and were produced, as I under- l it, as a limited edition of around 100 n.

'he plates are twelve inches (dinner and are etched in sepia on white. In enter there is the Stacy Tollman etching e Van Wickle Gates. . .on the top bor- the Brown University seal.

Vhen I graduated from Brown (1935) nother gave me one dozen of these plates. Several years later, Tilden Thurber notified her that they were discontinuing the sale of these plates, and she bought several dozen to use as wedding and graduation presents for Brown friends and children of these friends. My brother, Nörden Schloss '39, has a dozen and mother kept a dozen for herself.

Recently, at age 90, mother (wife of Berrick Schloss '04) closed her apartment and moved into a retirement home. While she does have some of her possessions with her, her space is limited and it was necessary to divide the important pieces among her children and grandchildren. At the moment, I have her dozen of the Spode Brown plates and I might consider selling them to someone who would want them for their collector's value, price to be negotiated. I do have a minimum (set by a local antique dealer) and will be happy to discuss the sale with anyone who wishes to write to me about it (2760 Banyan Rd., Apt. A-4, Boca Raton 33432).

DOROTHY SCHLOSS SHUTT '35
Boca Raton, Fla.

Reunion remembrances... Commencement gifts...

Now you can own — or give — beautiful Wedgwood with scenes from College Hill.

These handsome plates serve as a conversation-making memento of Brown and its landmarks. They're wonderful for gift-giving or simply as a treat for your own table.

Measuring a full 10½" diameter on Wedgwood's own creamware, struck in sepia, the set is a re-issue of an earlier, popular offer, now sold-out. As Wedgwoods alone, the plates are a remarkable value; as souvenirs of Brown years, they are collectors' items.

These Queen's Ware plates are available individually at $30 each, or you can save $40 by ordering a full set of eight. You can order all of one scene, if you wish. But do order now. First-come, first-served. We've made it easy to order by arranging for VISA or MasterCard charges.

.ssociated Alumni
ox 1859, Brown University
rovidence, RI 02912

Make checks payable to Associated Alumni of Brown University

e plates: $30 plus $1.75 shipping and insurance
f eight: $200 plus $5 shipping and insurance

______ CLASS YEAR OR PARENT

______ T ADDRESS

______ ;TATE, ZIP

ject of the Associated Alumni of Brown University.

____ Full set of 8 plates, each a different scene @ $205 $____

Individual plates as noted:

____ 1 VAN WICKLE GATES @$31.75 ____
____ 2 PEMBROKE HALL @$31.75 ____
____ 3 FIRST BAPTIST MEETING HOUSE @$31.75 ____
____ 4 JOHN NICHOLAS BROWN GATE @$31.75 ____
____ 5 MANNING HALL @$31.75 ____
____ 6 SOLDIERS ARCH @$31.75 ____
____ 7 WRISTON QUAD @$31.75 ____
____ 8 HOPE COLLEGE @$31.75 ____

TOTAL ENCLOSED $____

☐ I wish to pay by VISA/MasterCard. My account number is ____ and the expiration date is ____

______ signature

Twist and Shout!

"Left foot, green!" "Right hand, blue!" A collective groan arose from several hundred student contortionists in what was billed as "The World's Largest Twister Game." Sponsored by the Grass Roots main campus coordinators, the event was part of a Thursday afternoon Spring Weekend kickoff on April 28. Milton-Bradley, Twister's manufacturer, donated 100 plastic playing boards; taped together, they formed a technicolor rug on the Green in front of University Hall.

The Twisting lasted from 3 p.m. until 5:30; the students' endurance, no doubt, was enhanced by a mass ice-cream chowdown ("the world's largest sundae," served in a trough traversing the Green). But because of a technicality, the Twister game won't be in the *Guinness Book of World Records*. That's okay; "we just wanted to sponso[r] something really crazy," says Linda Segal '83 of the Grass Roots committee.

Maybe the best part was near the end, when the spinners called out, "Okay—HUG ANYBODY!" A great cheer went up; everyone dove and rolled into clinches. A rock band bega[n] to set up in front of Sayles; Spring Weekend was under way.

A Greek chorus of students, faculty, and staff shouted directions (below) to the Twister-players.

Photographs by John Forasté

IN THE NEWS:

By 1989, a computer for everyone on campus?

The computer age is not merely dawning at Brown; it may soon be high noon. A proposal under consideration would spend $50 to $70 million in the next six years to equip each faculty member, student, administrator, and staff member on campus with a powerful new type of personal computer.

A fifty-one-page proposal describing the experiment is circulating among the faculty and Corporation, and it describes the way the University will "migrate" from its current system of time-sharing accounts on a large mainframe computer to a system of personal computers connected to each other through the Brown University Network (BRUNET). But "this isn't simply an effort to develop a 'wired campus,' " says William Shipp, associate provost for computing. "We want to study the way scholars work—what they do and how they do it—and create a computing environment which lets them devise new ways to enrich and increase their work."

Experiments will lead to the development of the "scholar's workstation"—and the term scholar includes faculty, students, and staff—a package of computing tools that lies at the heart of the proposed project. In the beginning, the workstations will provide secretarial functions, such as electronic mail, conferencing, calendars, word processing, filing, and other automated functions that are available now. Soon, as libraries and other databases become accessible to computers, the workstation could be used more like a research assistant. Scholars could easily instruct the computer to gather data, plot charts and graphs, search journals, organize research notes, or prepare bibliographies.

"This system is going to fundamentally change the way we work," Shipp says. "Right now computers are not all that useful—you have to adapt your workstyle to the way the computer has been programmed. There is also the need to conserve computing power. We've all had to make compromises with the system we have now." New developments in personal computer software promise to relieve some of the alienating aspects of computer use—complicated, "user-hostile" methods of operation. In some new machines, a single set of simple procedures operates all parts of the computer, from word processing to data management to sketching and graphics. An entire system can be learned in thirty minutes.

Workstations will develop different capabilities for different academic departments and will provide instructional as well as research functions. "We will be building kits that you can tailor to your needs," Shipp says. "We will be going to the people in the English department, the classics department, to work with them and find out what kind of tools they need. The style of computing we're talking about will allow people to make adaptations. The editor of the *BAM*, for instance, will never want to make maximum use of a computer until he has a system that will allow him to see what an entire layout page looks like. Until there are data bases as useful to people as notecards, that you can manipulate and rearrange, the computer won't be very useful. The millenium is not here, however. All these things won't happen overnight. What we have now is the opportunity to help people build the tools, help them adapt them to their needs."

Different disciplines would be able to find special applications for their workstations. Advanced graphics can provide on-line source materials that do not use the Roman alphabet—musical notation, Sanskrit, Greek, and Hebrew, for example. High-resolution color graphics will enable musicians to call up entire orchestral scores; artists could develop and refine a full-color electronic sketch pad or use the computer to study color and three-dimensional design.

The project is distinguished by its strongly experimental philosophy. Brown's purpose is not to act primarily as a developer of these new software systems; rather it plans to act as a critical consumer. It would use new prod-

RESEARCH:

High-tech partnership is a first for Brown

"One. (Pause.) Two. (Pause.) Three. (Pause.)."

Les Niles Sc.M. '83 is speaking into a microphone held in place by a headset; simultaneously he is typing each word into a computer terminal. "Hello. (Pause.) Good morning." On a screen resembling a television set to his right, Niles's spoken words are being charted in living color: Each consonant and vowel, each nuance of tone, pitch, and timbre, is represented by a series of staggered vertical lines.

The technology Niles is demonstrating, here in a corner of a laboratory in Brown's Barus & Holley Building, is not just a pretty toy, a grown-up's version of "Speak and Spell." It is a bulky working model of a more refined system that will be produced and marketed by a new Providence firm called Sphere Technology, Inc.—a firm whose affiliation with Brown marks the University's first formal partnership with a profit-making company.

California has Silicon Valley; Boston is girdled by the many high-technology firms clustered along Route 128. In both instances, the development of high-tech companies is a direct outgrowth of university laboratories such as those at Stanford and MIT. Rhode Island has lagged behind, despite state officials' attempts to woo high-tech industry (which could help alleviate the state's high rate of unemployment). But Sphere's brand of cooperation between industry and University may be the beginning of a grass-roots solution to Rhode Island's economic woes, as well as a potentially lucrative venture for Sphere's officers and for Brown. The latter possibility stems from an agreement between Sphere and Brown: In exchange for commercial rights to this particular technology developed in Brown's laboratory, Sphere is giving Brown an undisclosed number of shares in the privately-held firm. The University has estimated that those shares could someday be worth $1 million or more.

Sphere will produce sophisticated computer systems that recognize words spoken by human voices. The masterminds behind the high-technology product—one in which businesses around the country have expressed interest—are Professor of Engineering Harvey Silverman '71 Ph.D., director of the Laboratory for Engineering Man/Machine Systems (LEMS), and Jeffrey Weiss, a visiting research assistant. Both are former IBM researchers who decided several years ago to market the advanced speech-recognition system they were working on at Brown.

"Others are doing speech-recognition work," Silverman says. But to date, he says, other systems are neither efficient to use nor inexpensive. "This will be the first that's easy, cheap, and that will work well." Les Niles, who already is employed by Sphere's engineering department, agrees: "The relatively small size, the cost, and the user-friendliness of our system are important advantages," he says, "but the key point is that we will deliver

Sphere's Jeffrey Weiss, William Kirk, and Harvey Silverman.

good performance."

In addition, Sphere is different from some of the larger firms working on speech recognition—among them Texas Instruments and Exxon—in that it will limit its marketing to a very specific target. "We are addressing IBM business computer users," explains Weiss. "These are businesses that involve lots of form-filling: insurance records, accounts payable, that sort of thing. It will assist employees, such as managers, who may not know how to type, or who are resisting using a computer system." Not only will such people feel comfortable dictating data into their terminals, they also will save time—the data will not require transcription by a clerical employee.

Working in Sphere's headquarters about a mile from Brown on Richmond Street, Weiss and his engineering staff are now assembling the first of the actual devices that will be sold. The machine will be "the size of a briefcase, or smaller," Silverman believes. Weiss is less specific about the product's finished appearance—"We're still building it," he says—but emphasizes that it will be relatively unobtrusive. The device will be integrated with the user's existing terminal. "It will allow the user both to use the keyboard and to speak directly to the machine," Weiss says.

In about a year, Sphere will begin selling its product and expects actual delivery to take place within fifteen or sixteen months from now. With seven employees, Sphere is still small, but Weiss already is interviewing more technical people. "We'll have a nucleus of scientists and engineers," he says, "but within a few years our workforce could grow to several hundred, including manufacturing people, sales people, and office staff." (In a *Providence Journal* article in early April, Silverman was more exuberant: "We expect to be the biggest employer in Rhode Island," he exclaimed.)

A company like Sphere was but a gleam in Silverman's and Weiss's eyes until William Kirk got involved. Kirk, an engineer who left his native England because of its scant opportunities for advancement, was most recently vice president for marketing of Gulton Industries in Rhode Island. He had given some thought to changing jobs, to going out on his own in business. He had no idea, however, that his friend Harvey Silverman might be a key to such a venture—no idea, even, that Silverman was an engineering whiz doing pioneering work with computers at Brown.

"Harvey and I had known each other for two years," says Kirk in his quick, lightly-accented British/American, "playing bridge with the New Neighbors Club in East Greenwich."

"One night after a volleyball game," Silverman chimes in, "I mentioned to Bill that Jeff and I wanted to start a company. From that time on, we couldn't shake Bill. He really went out on the longest limb for this project."

Kirk spent every spare moment planning the business aspects of Sphere: doing marketing research, preparing presentations for venture capitalists. Last year Silverman asked Brown Trustee Frank Wezniak '54 to get involved; he provided advice on pulling together a total business plan.

Last June 1, Kirk made his first presentations to "three or four" venture capitalists in Boston. "They were prestigious firms, but on the conservative side—we got a lot of 'call us laters.' By August we had decided what we needed was a venture capitalist who had lots of money, an affinity for high-technology arrangements, and who was willing to take a risk on a start-up." Through a contact at Northeastern, Kirk came up with Morgan Holland, a company that fortuitously closed its own fund in September. "Morgan Holland did three months of research into us," Kirk says, "and into our connection with Brown. The week before Christmas, they said they would fund us."

The venture-capital firm was concerned, Kirk said, about certain aspects of the project's administration. So an administration was put together: Kirk is president ("I've never been a CEO before," he exclaims happily), Weiss is director of engineering, and Wezniak is chairman of the board. Silverman, because of his Brown faculty appointment, cannot be a Sphere officer but is serving as a technical advisor. All are major stockholders.

With $1.7 million in backing already promised to the firm, Sphere has made a solid start in the high-tech arena. And Brown has dipped its toe into waters other research universities have plunged into for several years. "There have been other collaborations with industry discussed at Brown," says Provost Maurice Glicksman, "mostly in the medical field. Most of the standard

to tackle the tough job of handling the financial challenges that face Brown in the years ahead," said President Swearer. "We're delighted that he has chosen to bring his experience to the service of Brown; I am confident that we have found the right person for this most important position." K.H.

SABBATICALS:

Provost Glicksman takes a year off

JOHN FORASTÉ

A motion has been made and seconded at a faculty meeting. Discussion begins; a professor asks a question. Almost immediately a stocky man with curly black hair pops from his front-row seat in Carmichael Auditorium. "Mr. President, I'd like to address that, if I may. . ." And Provost Maurice Glicksman begins one of many elaborations he will provide on matters arising that afternoon.

"You know who could tell you more about that program?" a reporter is advised. "Call Maurie Glicksman."

Every college or university has one: The omnipresent dean or other senior administrator who keeps his or her finger on the institution's pulse, the person to whom inquiries about academic programs, historical background, and other topics are routinely referred. Such administrators pay a price for being perennially on top of the convoluted workings of a complex institution. It is difficult, if not impossible, for them to get away from campus for any significant amount of R&R.

Provost Maurice Glicksman is one such administrator. But after fourteen years at Brown, he is finally going to get his R&R—in this case, "Research and (some) Relaxation"—in the form of a one-year sabbatical. He will spend most of it in a laboratory at MIT, analyzing the results of experiments having to do with properties of condensed matter.

An engineer and physicist, Glicksman joined the Brown faculty in 1969 as University Professor and professor of engineering. He was already a widely respected researcher, having worked for fifteen years for RCA Research Laboratories in Princeton and Tokyo.

It wasn't long before his administrative talents were called into service at Brown, beginning with the chairmanship of the Faculty Policy Group. In 1974 Glicksman was named dean of the Graduate School. In 1975 he was appointed acting dean of the faculty and academic affairs, retaining his Graduate School responsibilities, and in 1976 he was named to the former deanship permanently, making him the University's chief academic officer.

Glicksman has been provost since 1978, when Merton Stoltz retired from the post. He has continued to teach occasional courses in his specialty—the properties of semiconductor alloys, materials used to make high-powered devices that give off light and energy. In addition, Glicksman acts in the president's stead whenever Howard Swearer is unavailable.

"I've worked fourteen years here without taking a sabbatical," says Glicksman. "I think I need a break from the routines, a chance to engage my intellectual capacities in a different direction." Perched on a long, formal sofa in his University Hall office, Glicksman regards a visitor steadily through a gray haze of smoke from his favorite prop, a large cigar.

Glicksman's cigars have seen him through fourteen years of extraordinary change and a measure of tumult at Brown. In 1975, as a member of the administration's negotiating team, he was credited by many observers with the successful resolution of grievances surrounding the Third World Coalition's occupation of University Hall. Around the same time, working on the

Maurice Glicksman: Ready for R&R.

JOHN FORASTÉ

controversial faculty staffing plan outlined in President Donald Hornig's "White Paper," Glicksman was able to lower the number of faculty to be cut from seventy-five to around twenty. (Doing so put constraints on faculty salary raises, however, and Glicksman was quick to thank a "remarkably dedicated faculty" for sticking by Brown through troubled times.)

More recently, Glicksman has shepherded the development of numerous programs, centers, and departments, taking particular pride in the strengthening of such areas as computer science, mathematics, and the cognitive sciences.

From his temporary apartment on the twenty-fifth floor of a building overlooking the Charles River at MIT, Glicksman may not be able to see all the way to College Hill next year. But his mind will stray there frequently, and he will be on campus one day a week. High on his list of concerns, he says, are the proposed installation of a network of computer workstations; a new cycle of academic program review and planning, to be directed by Associate Provost James Patterson; and an emphasis on foreign studies and international exchange programs.

"There are some skeptics among my colleagues," Glicksman says with a grin and a puff of cigar smoke, "who insist that I'm not going to get a break, that I'll be too close to Brown, too involved. But I made the choice to do my research at MIT because I felt I wanted to maintain a continuity here. I believe that cutting myself off completely from Brown at this stage would not be in the best interests of the University. And, I plan to return to Brown refreshed and ready to get back to work."

In Glicksman's absence, no acting provost will be named. His responsibilities will be distributed, instead, among the associate provosts, deans, and the president. Glicksman will continue to chair the Academic Council and Committee on Faculty Reappointment and Tenure. *A.D.*

STUDENTS:

Cleaning up the Green for financial aid

At 7:30 in the morning, the calm that hangs over the Green is palpable. A dog barks, a cardinal whistles, an early employee walks slowly down the

The volunteers (Larry Siff in white pants in the cent

sidewalk, cup of steaming coffee in hand. The campus is self-absorbed and collected.

But wait! What sight from yonder arches breaks? A student. No, two students, three! And they're carrying—trash bags? Soon the Green is covered with a score of students harvesting another crop of litter. This is Keep Brown Beautiful at work.

Since early March, students, not Plant Operations, have accepted the responsibility for keeping the campus clean. The idea for a Keep Brown Beautiful program was conceived by Larry Siff '84, who was serving as vice president of the student government last year when he decided to do something about the enormous amounts of litter left over after the bacchanal of Spring Weekend. "I've always felt a sense of social responsibility," Siff explains. "I like to think about what I can do to improve Brown. Last year, a week and a half before Spring Weekend I started thinking about the garbage on the Green and how no one takes the responsibility for cleaning it up except Plant Operations. So I got about eighty students and President Swearer to come out on Sunday morning of Spring Weekend and clean up. We collected almost 3,000 pounds of trash," he recalls proudly.

When he saw that there were students—and administrators—who cared enough about the campus to clean it

they never litter. We are after the people who *do* litter. We want to stop litter. Period." *K.H.*

JOHN FORASTE

ur to $8. The endowment fund appeals to everyone, as Siff says, "No e is pro-litter and anti-financial aid. is is also showing people outside own that we care. We care about autifying the campus and about en- ring diversity here."

Every morning there are an average twenty students out picking up cigarette butts, beer and pop cans, and per in the bushes, streets, and sidewalks. Keep Brown Beautiful has also read to the surrounding community, d Siff has organized the merchants Thayer Street, many of whom serve the board of KBB. President vearer has remarked that "it's an pressive sight to walk across the Green at 8 in the morning and see students out cleaning it up. Of course it would be even more impressive if it weren't littered to begin with."

Keep Brown Beautiful was certified by Keep America Beautiful on April 25, making Brown the first university in the country to achieve this status. But Siff isn't satisfied. "Keep Brown Beautiful is not a one-shot deal; it can't depend on one person to keep it going. We have to make people feel a sense of ownership about this place, they have to feel part of it. People can't feel as though they're just visiting, that if we litter someone else will clean up after us. So many of the people who come out every morning to clean up say that

SPORTS

By Peter Mandel

MEN'S LACROSSE:

The numbers are getting better

With a little more than two-thirds of the season gone, men's lacrosse was juggling numbers. The team had racked up its highest victory total since 1980 (seven), and its longest win streak since 1971 (six straight). "We have beaten excellent teams and we have done it on the road and at home, and in all kinds of weather," Coach Dom Starsia remarked. "We deserve a good ranking." Before Brown fell to Ivy contender Penn on April 23, the Bruins were ranked tenth in the nation.

Some other numbers: Goaltender Marcus Woodring '83 had a 7-2 record and a 7.72 goals-against average, impressive statistics in the often high scoring game of lacrosse.

Freshman Tom Gagnon led the team with a remarkable 23 goals and 16 assists. His attack-mate, Mick Matthews '85 had 12 goals and 17 assists, and another freshman, John Keogh, had 8 and 13, respectively. The statisticians pulled out their pocket calculators and determined that Brown had outshot its opponents 38 to 35 per game, and outscored them by an average of almost three goals.

Not bad for an attack that was considered something of an unknown quantity before the season began.

The Bruin defense had done its job with equal determination, especially in the 7-2 victory over the University of Massachusetts and the 8-4 defeat of Princeton. Led by Bill Aliber '83 who has a chance to become the first three-time All-Ivy Brown lacrosseman, it was considered one of the stronger defensive units in Division I—allowing six goals or fewer on six different occasions. Against Harvard and the University of New Hampshire, Aliber allowed the leading scorers among the enemy a total of two assists.

MEN'S CREW:

Knocking off the national champion

Men's crew began the dual-meet season this year with a mix of the expected and the unexpected.

No one was surprised when the crew won its first race on April 9 against Boston University and Coast Guard. The varsity boat was expected to do well—Brown had handily defeated these schools in 1982 for two of its three wins. So when the Bruins rowed to easy victory and a course record on the Seekonk, onlookers cheered and went home satisfied that God was in his heaven and all was as it should be in the world of college crew.

But rowing is not a predictable sport: Only in England do they wager on it.

Before the season, Coach Steve Gladstone had expected Brown to be strong, though he had been somewhat guarded in his predictions. "The league is tight in terms of speed," he had said. "As many as nine crews have a reasonable shot at winning the Easterns and the IRAs this spring."

What he didn't dare predict, and what fans along the Housatonic didn't bet on, was for the Brown crew to knock off last year's national champion on April 10 by slightly more than two seconds. The fact that the national champion happened to be Yale, and that this was the first-ever dual meet between the two, made for added drama.

Yale, which was coming off a convincing win over Dartmouth, took a 3/4 length advantage in the first 100 meters. The Brown boat began to gain steadily, and pulled even with about 500 meters to go on the 2000-meter course. Led by coxswain Chris Snell, the Bruins edged out to a 2/3 of a length lead and held it to the finish.

This was Yale's first loss to an American college crew in two years, and the *Providence Journal* trumpeted, "The. . .race proved that Brown belongs in the front rank of Eastern college crews." "It was a wonderful victory for us," added Gladstone. "The guys were determined to work hard for those big wins this season."

Unfortunately, the Bruins could not make their momentum last the month of April. Choppy conditions on the Charles contributed to a Harvard triumph on April 16, and a determined Northeastern crew outsprinted Brown on the Seekonk a week later. With only a dual race with Dartmouth remaining before the Eastern Sprints in mid-May, Gladstone was forced to do some "re-evaluating" with an eye toward improving on last year's fifth-place finish.

SCOREBOARD

(April 3 through May 7)

Baseball (13-15-1)
Brown 4, Morehead State 3
Morehead State 2, Brown 0
Liberty Baptist 3, Brown 2
Navy 5, Brown 1
Navy 6, Brown 5
Princeton 12, Brown 10
Brown 3, Princeton 3
Brown 5, Massachusetts 3
Massachusetts 4, Brown 3
Penn 5, Brown 0
Penn 8, Brown 5
Brown 7, Columbia 2
Brown 6, Columbia 2
Brown 14, Cornell 7
Brown 7, Cornell 3
Brown 9, Army 4
Brown 13, Army 0
Holy Cross 5, Brown 0
Providence 7, Brown 3
Brown 4, Harvard 1
Harvard 6, Brown 4
Northeastern 8, Brown 3
Northeastern 7, Brown 0
Brown 13, Holy Cross 3

Men's Crew (4-2)
Brown 5:39.0, Boston University 5:46.3, Coast Guard 5:52.0
Brown 5:56.8, Yale 5:59.1
Harvard 6:10.5, Brown 6:15.7
Northeastern 6:23.0, Brown 6:27.4
Brown over Dartmouth, 3 lengths

Women's Crew (4-4)
Harvard 5:07.0, Brown 5:10.0, MIT 5:27.0, Northeastern 5:33.0
Brown 5:14.5, Rutgers 5:17.3
Smith 5:33.2, Brown 5:34.1

Men's Golf (6-5)
Brown 374, Bryant 377, Bentley 379 Babson 400
Brown 413, Yale 422, Columbia 427
Providence 389, Rhode Island 394, Brown 401
4th in Ivy Championships
Providence 383, Brown 389, Holy Cross 396
7th of 15 at New England Championships
Harvard 385, Brown 386
Dartmouth 375, Brown 388

Men's Lacrosse (9-5)
Brown 10, Harvard 5
Brown 13, New Hampshire 10
Brown 7, Massachusetts 2
Brown 8, Princeton 4
Penn 16, Brown 8
Brown 11, Yale 2
Dartmouth 5, Brown 4
Brown 13, Cornell 7

Women's Lacrosse (3-7)
Dartmouth 8, Brown 6
Yale 17, Brown 4
Cornell 9, Brown 5
Harvard 14, Brown 6
Princeton 17, Brown 3
Brown 17, Holy Cross 3
Brown 15, Boston University 9

Women's Softball (16-11)
Brown 6, Furman 1
Brown 5, Furman 3
South Carolina-Spartanburg 4, Brown 3
Brown 14, South Carolina-Spartanburg 10
Stonehill 3, Brown 2
Brown 2, Stonehill 1
Providence 4, Brown 0
Providence 1, Brown 0
Brown 15, Barrington 8
Brown 11, Barrington 1
2nd in Ivy Championships
Brown 5, Roger Williams 4
Brown 6, Roger Williams 0
Brown 8, Bridgewater State 7
Bridgewater State 7, Brown 6
Rhode Island College 8, Brown 2
Brown 4, Rhode Island College 1
Providence 6, Brown 1

Men's Tennis (14-4)
San Diego 7, Brown 2
Brown 5, California-Santa Barbara 4
Brown 6, Navy 3
Princeton 5, Brown 1
Brown 8, Boston University 1
Brown 6, Cornell 1
Brown 7, Army 2
Brown 8, Providence 1
Brown 6, Dartmouth 3
Harvard 7, Brown 2
Brown 5, Columbia 4
Brown 6, Rhode Island 0
3rd of 10 in New England Champions

Women's Tennis (7-7)
California-Santa Barbara 9, Brown 0
California-Irvine 8, Brown 1
Brown 7, Cal State-Los Angeles 2
Brown 6, Cal State-Northridge 3
Penn 9, Brown 0
Princeton 7, Brown 2
Yale 7, Brown 2
Brown 9, Cornell 0
Harvard 7, Brown 2
Brown 5, Rhode Island 1
Dartmouth 8, Brown 1
Brown 7, Massachusetts 2

Men's Track (2-3)
Harvard 87, Dartmouth 64 1/2, Brown 51 1/2
Rhode Island 83, Brown 72
7th in Heptagonal Championships

Women's Track (4-1)
Harvard 72 1/2, Brown 55 1/2, Dartmouth 31
4th in Heptagonal Championships

It is always Old Brown and it is always New Brown. I am here to greet the New Brown of this era, to hail the dawning of a new day full of the brightest promise.

CHARLES EVAN HUGHES 1881
at Commencement 1937

IN CELEBRATION

Chief Justice Hughes's words are probably more applicable today than they were even in 1937. At that time, a new president, Henry M. Wriston, was about to launch Brown's evolution from a small, regional institution to a nationally recognized university. In 1983, Howard Swearer leads an internationally known university, which, as a result of the momentum set in motion by the establishment of the new curriculum in 1969, is now among the nation's most popular institutions with the talented students it seeks. Furthermore, the University is completing an unbelievably successful capital campaign. The goal five years ago was $158 million. As of May 15, receipts and pledges totaled $170 million, an amount that even the most optimistic would not have thought possible.

It seems appropriate to celebrate—and celebrate we do in this special issue. We're celebrating Brown University and we're celebrating the Campaign—and what the Campaign's success means for Brown's faculty and students.

We asked President Swearer to describe what the Campaign means for Brown in the coming years. His article begins on the next page. Eight members of the faculty have received endowed chairs as a result of the Campaign. We asked three of those eight to write an essay about some aspect of this University. Following the president's article, you will find an essay by Henry Kucera, the Fred M. Seed Professor of Linguistics and the Cognitive Sciences, a chair made possible by a gift from the Fred M. Seed Foundation of Minneapolis. James Seed '63 is the son of the late Fred Seed. On page 40, there is an essay by John Rowe Workman, the William Duncan Macmillan '53 Professor of Classics. The chair is the gift of the man for whom it is named. And on page 46, you will find an essay by Michael Harper, the I. J. Kapstein Professor of English. The chair, named for the popular retired professor of English and member of the class of '26, was made possible by a gift from Marvyn Carton '38.

To celebrate visually, we asked John Forasté to provide us with a photo essay in color (it begins on page 24) and illustrator Valerie Marsella to sketch some of the buildings constructed or renovated with gifts to the Campaign.

We hope you enjoy the issue—and join us in celebration.

—The Editors

Future generations will judge the true meaning of the Campaign for Brown's contribution to the University's eminence not so much by what was just concluded, but by

WHAT THE CAMPAIGN BEGAN

By Howard R. Swearer

The announcement in the autumn of 1978 of the $158-million Campaign for Brown was an act of commitment—and no little faith. There was no way then to "know" if such a sum could be raised. If recent experience with fund-raising had been a guide, the prospects were grim. However, those close to the University knew that the Campaign simply *had* to succeed, for failure would have serious consequences for the quality and character of Brown. This was not a discretionary effort but one central to the University's well-being.

Nor could we delay in starting the Campaign in order to engage in more thorough preparations and planning. It is no exaggeration, I believe, to assert that if an effort of this magnitude had not been launched when it was and carried through successfully in a timely manner, the University would have been faced with painful decisions about its size, configuration, and missions that could well have resulted in distinctly altered institutional directions. Without it, Brown could not possibly have enjoyed the favorable position it does today.

While the enhanced stream of gift revenue generated by the Campaign was critical, there were other important purposes and benefits as well. They need to be widely understood if Brown is to realize full measure from this strenuous five-year effort in which so many were involved and to which so many contributed generously. It needs to be appreciated that this was not a one-shot affair which, now successfully concluded, can be forgotten after an appropriate round of congratulatory celebrations. In fact, the Campaign has been the centerpiece of a series of activities to put in place the structures, procedures, and disciplines required to build and maintain Brown's strengths.

During the early and mid-1970s, the major preoccupation of the administration and the Corporation was to reduce costs in order to bring income and expenditures into balance. Although the University had lived beyond its means for over a decade, there was, in fact, little "fat" to be eliminated; budget reductions were, therefore, painful and oftentimes contentious. It was essential, nonetheless, to end the erosion of quasi (unrestricted) endowment and to demonstrate to the Brown community that the University could live by the discipline of a balanced operating budget. After more than a decade of deficits, the goal was finally achieved during the first year of the Campaign for Brown and has since been sustained. There is little doubt that this achievement had a highly positive effect on the course of the Campaign—and it was important to accomplish before the Campaign moved into high gear.

It is proper for the University to be lean and trim, but the budgetary restrictions of the 1970s were threatening to weaken its institutional muscle: A new infusion of revenue was essential. After several years of paring down programs and delaying plans for various institutional improvements, morale was beginning to sag. We recognized the core assumption that academic priorities must shape budget decisions and not the reverse. But, because the means were not available to support various faculty initiatives, there was little motivation to propose initiatives. Too much energy was spent on warding off reductions to think positively and

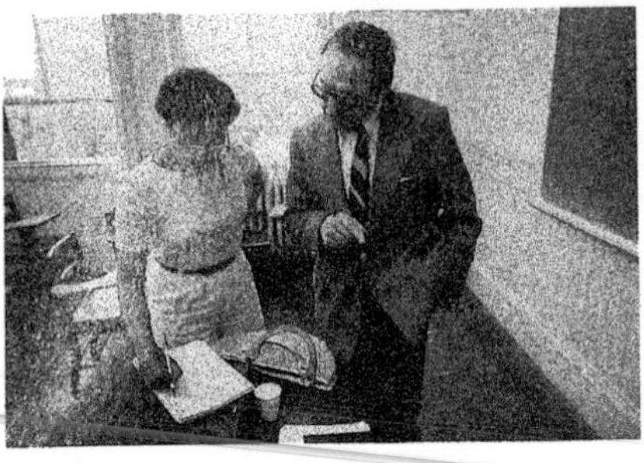

JOHN FORASTÉ

creatively about the future. Desperately needed additions and improvements to facilities had already been postponed for too long. In short, the climate was not conducive to maximizing existing strengths, let alone planning to enhance them in the future.

Preparations for the Campaign provided the context and the motivation for longer-range planning. In cooperation with departments, academic needs were reviewed and projected forward. Space and facilities requirements were studied, and a comprehensive plan for improvements and additions was developed. Departments were encouraged to raise their vision. It was understood that the primary direction of the Campaign had to be toward strengthening the fundamental foundations of the University and that "budget add-ons" would have to be judicious and selective; nonetheless, our planning had changed from budget reductions to the possibility of some additional resources for especially pressing and attractive activities. Anyone one who has ever engaged in institutional planning knows that the latter context provides for a planning process that is more thoughtful, participatory, open—honest.

As it should, this healthy ferment has continued. Moreover, a number of faculty members and departments have been active participants in the quest to seek funding for their projects (and for the Campaign in general). Since they are the most persuasive advocates for Brown's teaching and research programs, the Campaign could not have succeeded without their direct involvement. And, I am happy to say, this willingness by many faculty members to search out support shows no sign of abating—a lasting benefit of the Campaign.

Many tangible benefits have flowed from the Campaign—in teaching and research programs and improved facilities—ranging across the entire spectrum of the University. They are too numerous to describe here. However, the Campaign also has had a more generalized effect on attitudes and atmosphere. As the Campaign built momentum and confidence grew, we became more adventuresome and willing to take prudent risks. At a time when many other institutions were adopting a defensive posture, Brown was aggressively pushing forward on many fronts ranging across computing and computer science, women's studies, a public policy program, gerontology, chemical engineering, and many others. Previously existing programs of outstanding quality, from population studies to geology, enhanced their winning ways. Old buildings were renovated and new facilities were constructed on a fast track to minimize the inroads of inflation.

The momentum—the sense of excitement as milestones were reached—unified, in a most positive way, this institution that prides itself on its diversity. The Students Campaign for Brown Committee, a grassroots group, assumed its own responsibility for spreading the Campaign word on campus. Their presence and initiative were obvious. And when the bells in Carrie Tower sounded to announce reaching the $100 million mark, the emotion was palpable. Staff and volunteers, whose dedication to Brown and hard work during the Campaign cannot be overestimated—and can certainly never be sufficiently praised—were infused with a second wind. Analogous to the runner's high, each new success spurred greater effort. And with this spirit we were able to reach the Campaign goal six months early.

Thus far, I have discussed the impact of the Campaign on the campus. Its effect on the University's relations with external constituencies has been no less profound. It was the powerful stimulus for us to get to know our alumni, parents, and friends; to communicate more intensely and earnestly than ever before; to encourage the organization of various alumni activities and events. What we discovered was a welling up of enthusiasm and good will for Brown and a ready willingness to be of help and to be involved. The reservoir of pride in, and loyalty to, the University was broader and deeper than we had dared to imagine. The bonds of the Brown community were tightened.

When "Brown Has Arrived" banners went up in cities all over the country announcing the various Campaign kickoffs, we were making a

JOHN FORASTÉ

profound statement indeed. Brown *had* arrived, bringing faculty, administrators, and staff to spread the word that this campus was alive and well and in the front line of research and scholarship. And Brown had arrived to take its place in that small circle of first-rank institutions looked to as flagbearers in education.

The Brown degree has always had high value. The quality and loyalty of our alumni and alumnae prove over and over again that the years spent on College Hill affected their lives in strong, positive ways. But even the most chauvinistic among us must recognize Brown's new visibility and increased prestige.

These lessons must not be forgotten in the post-Campaign period. Brown's greatness rests in large measure on the loyalty and support of those who believe in the value of Brown's mission—to themselves and to society. We, together, have demonstrated to ourselves what can be achieved; and the strengthened ties that made it all happen must be constantly renewed.

Brown has been moving quickly these last five years. It would be tempting to take a rest, to relax and read the press clippings. Such an indulgence we cannot afford. To lose the momentum gained over the last half decade would be a strategic error.

We take very seriously the new responsibility that comes with increased prominence. Popularity is ephemeral. But Brown intends to continue to merit the attention it has achieved. This University offers a superb education to some of the most motivated students in the country. Here, faced with many challenging alternatives, they learn to make wise decisions. How they make those choices, how they learn, may be as important as what they learn.

Brown, too, as an institution, will have choices to make. We have seen major changes in the five years since the Campaign began, and we anticipate the emergence of many new directions in the years ahead. We must be ready enough, and flexible enough, to make and to support financially the choices the future will offer.

The Campaign could not address many of the priority needs of the University (after the first round of planning in early 1978, the cost of the projects judged meritorious totaled some three times the final Campaign goal of $158 million). Moreover, the Campaign itself generated new opportunities for Brown. In short, much remains to be accomplished—as should always be the case for a vigorous, healthy institution.

A prime purpose of the Campaign was not simply to meet the five-year target but to raise dramatically the level of gifts to the University year in and year out. In the five years prior to 1978, the University received a total of $41 million in gifts from all sources for an average of $8.2 million annually. This level of gift income was well below Brown's capacity and was not commensurate with its stature and character. It also compared quite unfavorably with the records of other private universities of Brown's size and nature.

Our intention has been to exit from the Campaign with annual gift levels some three times higher than the pre-Campaign period and to sustain and increase them in the years ahead. Although the modes for encouraging support will change, the structures, attitudes, and intensity of effort developed over the last five years must not be permitted to erode. The Brown Fund must continue to grow and the endowment must continue to be strengthened on trajectories established during the course of the Campaign. A number of academic programs, computing, medical education, financial aid for undergraduate and graduate students, continued improvement of facilities, and more require additional funding.

The widespread sense of forward movement and the stature enjoyed by Brown have contributed immeasurably to the success of the Campaign; and, as I have suggested, the reverse is also true. This symbiotic relationship must be continually nurtured. We can all take pride in the success of the Campaign. But future generations will judge the true measure of its contribution to Brown's eminence not so much by what was successfully concluded this year, but by what the Campaign commenced. It should be regarded as a foundation rather than a capstone.

ENTAL WALLS

Brown's non-proprietary academic spirit encourages new fields and interdisciplinary exploration

By Henry Kučera

Like other universities, Brown has academic departments, some thirty of them—not counting various centers and programs. They offer courses, design concentration programs, recommend faculty appointments, and negotiate their budgets with the administrators. But unlike those in many other institutions, the departmental boundaries at Brown—at least from my personal experience—are not high disciplinary walls difficult to scale. There is, and long has been, at the University more than a modicum of non-proprietary academic spirit that accommodates new interests and encourages interdisciplinary exploration.

In a very real sense, my own career at Brown—which spans twenty-eight years, five presidents, and innumerable deans—is, for better or for worse, an example of this liberal academic *Weltanschauung*. The editors of the *Brown Alumni Monthly* permitted (or even encouraged) me to be personal in these brief recollections, and I shall take full advantage of their generosity. To start with: My academic title at Brown at present may well be the longest in the history of the University—or at least is a good candidate for that record. I have recently been honored by being appointed the Fred M. Seed Professor of Linguistics and the Cognitive Sciences; in addition to that, I hold the titles of professor of Slavic languages, of linguistics, and of cognitive science, and that of director of the Institute for Cognitive and Neural Research.

All of this, of course, could easily be a mixed blessing. It is not too difficult for intellectually restless people—and I count myself among them—to become dilettantes, the proverbial jacks of all trades. Surely, one role of departments is to guard the quality of the faculty, to exercise the necessary peer judgment about colleagues' work, and to plan a rational and informed development of the field with whose instruction they are charged. President Barnaby Keeney, I recall, was always on guard against colorful interdisciplinary schemes when he presided, as the president did by the rules of the faculty, over the Committee on the Curriculum, which defined the academic policy of the institution. There are thus clearly two sides to the picture: Excessive departmental constraints and boundaries can result in immobility and lack of development of new fields of inquiry and of teaching. Too little academic structure, on the other hand, can erode standards and lead to dilettantish indulgences. While there are no absolutely perfect universities, Brown has been rather successful in avoiding both pitfalls, creating an atmosphere on this campus of interdisciplinary collaboration in those areas where some integration of knowledge can be fruitfully expected and new vistas thus opened up.

Changes in academia are not really as slow as one might think. In my lifetime, change has been remarkably rapid. The two academic fields in which I do most of my current work, linguistics and cognitive science, were not independent entities when I first started teaching. Scholars interested in language in a general sense, i.e., in the development of languages, their comparison and structures, were then housed—and often welcomed, to be sure—in various very specifically labeled departments or divisions, be it English, Romance, German, or Slavic, most of them dominated by men and women of primarily literary interests.

Brown—one of the pioneers—introduced its undergraduate concentration in linguistics in the late 1950s and established a Department of Linguistics in 1960. Cognitive science, of course, is an even much younger discipline. Whatever interest there was twenty or thirty years ago in human cognition, in a systematic inquiry into how humans learn, process information, and reason, was within the community of those psychologists who were not in the mainstream of the behaviorist school. Brown now has two centers dedicated to inquiry about the human brain and mind: the Center for Neural Sciences, which spans the interests of the medical physiologists and the theorists of memory models; and a Center for Cognitive Science, which includes among its members faculty from psychology, linguistics, computer science, anthropology, and even engineering. The Institute for Cognitive and Neural Research has as its main task a coordination of these activities. Our hope is that all of us interested in this exciting area of learning will find a common home—physically as well as academically. The University has allocated to the neural and cognitive sciences and to linguistics the vacated Metcalf Research Laboratory, where, perhaps a year from now, we will work, discuss, and dispute all together.

My first assignment at Brown was as professor of Russian and German. Actually, the "German" part was tacked on as something of an afterthought, rather characteristic of the entire process in those somewhat patriarchal days of the Wriston presidency. I was probably one of the last faculty members that Mr. Wriston hired—or had a direct hand in hiring. I had met the Brown president some years before, when Henry Wriston was on a visiting committee at Harvard's Russian Research Center and I was still a graduate student there. When an opportunity arose for someone with my skills at Brown, I got the call to submit my credentials and come for an interview—a call that, clearly, had something to do with Mr. Wriston's excellent memory. It turned out, however, that the position in question was a one-year replacement for Edward J. Brown, at that time the only professor of Russian at the University. Since I already had an appointment at Harvard, a one-year replacement position was really not a very attractive proposition. When this complication came to President Wriston's attention, it was solved literally in two hours: The chairman of the Division of Modern Languages was authorized to offer me a three-year contract and to define the position in some way to make me useful after the first year. I was thus made an assistant professor of German as well.

I actually taught German for a year or two after Professor Brown returned from his sabbatical and enjoyed it greatly. But I never experienced Mr. Wriston's presidency while on campus since he retired the very summer that my wife and I moved to Providence.

The years of Barnaby Keeney's rule—"rule" seems to me an appropriate term—were, of course, years of

joined the Brown faculty as professor of linguistics and English in 1962. Soon after he arrived here, Francis, with Twaddell's encouragement, started work on collecting a number of present-day American-English texts that could be used as resources for computer-based research in the English language. The total collection, when it was completed, amounted to more than one million words. I was the computer "consultant" to this project for which Francis had a research grant. Even then, of course, computers were pretty puny machines. Brown had acquired one of the latest, an IBM 7070, a "second-generation" computer; but when the time came to sort the one million words in order to construct a vocabulary list and a frequency analysis of the vocabulary, it took us fourteen uninterrupted hours of computer time as sole users of the machine (and no time-sharing then) to do the job. But it got done, and Francis and I have since published two books for which this research served as a database. The one-million-word collection of texts in computer form has become known as the "Brown Corpus" and has been used by several hundred researchers all over the world.

My interdisciplinary encounter of the next kind was with Leon Cooper, officially a professor of physics at Brown, and Ulf Grenander, a Swedish mathematician who had joined the Brown faculty on a permanent basis. Cooper's interest had gradually shifted from superconductivity, which had won him the Nobel Prize, to an interest in neural models and, especially, mathematically-based models of memory organization. Grenander had an interest in grammar and its probabilistic properties. One warm Saturday afternoon, the three of us met and discussed the problem of how children learn their first language.

This "first language acquisition" is a remarkable process indeed. All normal children accomplish it, relatively quickly and without much instruction, just by being exposed to a language environment. And yet they master what is a very complex structure, a system of communication with many levels and subtleties. The three of us discussed, quite informally—in the true Brown spirit—what kind of formal learning models one could construct to explain at least the basic process in the acquisition of language, which would be consistent with known facts and reasonable assumptions about human memory, its associative powers, and its ability to generalize. It is, of course, precisely this need for realistic models that is served so well by interdisciplinary studies and discussions. There lurks a danger for the lonely researcher who ventures into new areas to construct hypotheses that may well seem plausible from the narrow perspective of his field, but that may be quite incompatible with accepted assumptions in other fields dealing with the same phenomena from a different point of view.

The pleasant labor of that Saturday afternoon bore fruit: We started modeling what we called an "abduction algorithm" (nothing illegal here—our "abduction" was not from the verb "to abduct" but from "abduce"). Eventually, two doctoral dissertations and several publications resulted from the development of the model. When the Center for Neural Studies—later renamed Center for Neural Sciences—became established at the University, Cooper became its co-director; both Grenander and I have served on its executive committee since the beginning. And when Richard Millward and his colleagues in psychology, linguistics, and computer science established the Center for Cognitive Science, the participation in this exciting new area of investigating the "ultimate frontier"—the structure and function of the human brain—found an enlarged and very active body of men and women from a number of very diverse departments talking, discussing, and organizing lectures and writing grant proposals together.

God and the guardians of the University's budget willing, we all should be moving into our renovated quarters in the old Metcalf Research Lab sometime within the next year. Although we meet now for discussions and seminars, the physical proximity of a common building and the interaction that it will stimulate should provide still further insights and discoveries.

Brown is indeed a University without high departmental walls, and it is this fact that has allowed the development of new fields and their energetic activity. When we move into Metcalf, there will be no walls—only partitions. May that be symbolic of the future and of Brown's continuing enlightenment.

Brown Is a Timeless Place in Any Season

A photographic essay by John Forasté

The past, the present, and the future. . .

The Sciences Library opened in 1971.

e men's crew rows back to the boathouse after a win on the Seekonk.

Special Collections Librarian Mark Brown at work in the John Hay.

Listening to Professor of Applied Mathematics Walter Freiberger.

Her gloves wait for a Panda.

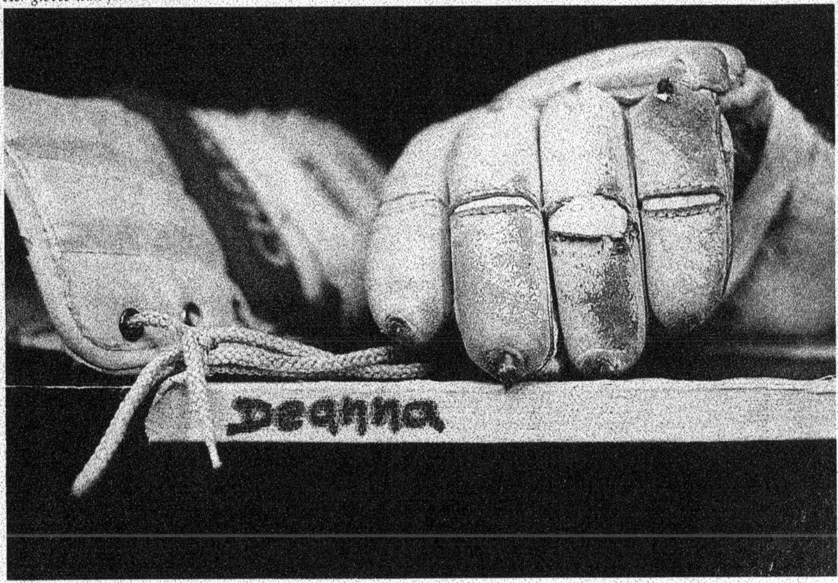

The beauty of spring outside the Rock.

The intensity of the classroom.

As it has grown and evolved over the years. . .

The basketball team upsets Penn in Marvel.

Outside, winter brings its own beauty to the Hill.

from a small New England college to an international University. . .

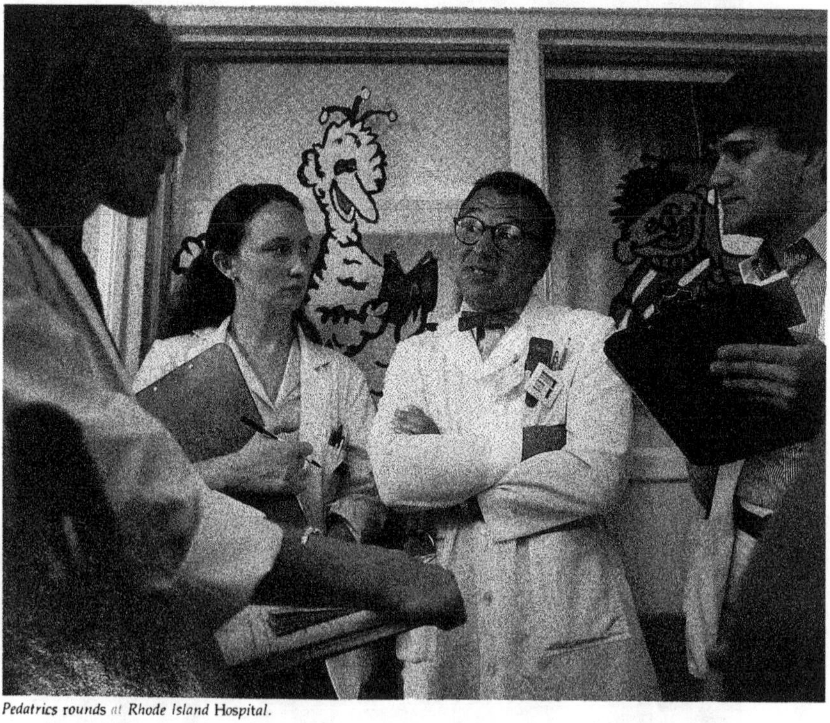

Pedatrics rounds at Rhode Island Hospital.

Chuck McGrath '83, who recently set a record for most wins in a Brown career.

Plantetary geologist Jim Head talks with a student.

Professor of Comparative Literature Karen Newman.

here the students *are*—*Faunce* House *mail boxes.*

Research is an integral part of a first-rank university.

And leisure is a necessary part of a student's life.

'ecent graduate both
hare in that heritage

You can't be sure what students are thinking while they are being lectured

ARE THEY GETTING THE MESSAGE?

—if perchance the people catch sight of a man renowned for goodness and worth, they become silent and stand by with attentive ears, as he with his speech sways their temper and soothes their hearts—

Vergil

By John Rowe Workman

Shortly before a fatal illness ended Alex Robinson's enthusiastic lectures on Greek history up in Alumnae Hall, he told me that he never lectured before undergraduates without thinking about what was going on in their minds. Their glazed eyes were fixed on the lectern; their faces indicated an expression of "show me"; their note-taking was as sporadic as it was industrious, depending upon the professor's emphasis; did they really comprehend the ingenuity of the Mycenaeans or the intricacies of Themistocles's ruse at Salamis? After all, there were organ pipes on either side of the stage to be counted; there was a memorial tablet above the door on the left of the stage that indicated a curious family situation or incest or both; would the sagging valance made of green velvet come crashing down on the professor? In the course of time, I began to share Alex's thoughts as I lectured from the same lectern. Do the students hear what is being said? Do they perceive the lecturer's interpretations? Does all this stimulate critical thinking?

Again, faculty chairs were at a premium in Sayles Hall when President Wriston gave the chapel address, and we went back again and again to hear that we must never fashion our lives to seek security or to learn that we must ask ourselves why the preparation for the problems of peace are never as thorough and as vigorous as they are for war. The faculty was thoughtful during these addresses, but what about the students? Did they take leave of their annoyance at compulsory chapel long enough to hear Wriston's admonitions? Did his dramatic rhetoric bestir their thoughts away from parietals? What about his plan to centralize fraternities in one quadrangle?

Once he learned not to drop his voice at the end of sentences, Barnaby Keeney delighted many of us with his perpetual call for a spirit of "divine discontent" about life, academic as well as political, and he did not need to cite an example from the thirteenth century to back up his point, which was simply stated. After all, Barney was one of our own. He thought like a professor. His illustrations, generally taken from his own life, revealed a deep understanding of humanity, the better as well as the worse, and we all waited for some "Keeneyism" to carry away from Sayl[es] or Alumnae. Students and professors alike listened and understood, and th[e] atmosphere of research and scholarsh[ip] was considerably enhanced. Still, the question remained: Would the studen[ts] continue their "divine discontent" aft[er] they left Brown and moved into the business and professional world?

In getting the message across we can never be sure how it will be received or the reaction it will evoke. In lectures students will find amusement at the most unlikely places. A perfectl[y] articulate lecture, complete with proof and impressive evidence, will be met with stony silence. It is a rare occasio[n] when a spectacular idea will arouse students; more likely there will be a response when a lapboard inadvertently falls on the floor or the pages of the *Hockey News* are flipped over somewhere in the back rows. If an opportunity for questions is given at the end of a lecture, there will invariably be one student who will ask the

very things pontificated from the platform during the preceding forty-eight minutes. Another student will ask three or four questions not particularly relevant to anything in the lecture or the subject at hand, questions yoked with the word "and."

Is it embarrassment that keeps these questions coming, rolling them up like Hannibal's victories as he moved down through central Italy against the Romans? It is to the credit of Rhode Island's Senator Claiborne Pell that he contended brilliantly with one of these compound-question merchants about a year ago in Alumnae Hall. Senator Pell had just finished a fine address on foreign policy before a packed audience of undergraduates. In the question period one of our campus politicos rose and posed a six-pronged question; that is, he asked six different questions in one sentence, none of them pertaining to the address and none of the questions related to each other. I suppose that persons in public life are tuned into this sort of thing. Professors are not.

The question may be raised whether lecturing is any longer a valid form of communication. Will discussion groups take over the transmission of knowledge (if indeed students have read enough of the text to participate in a discussion)? It is very easy to isolate, in a discussion, which students have read the assignment and which have not, but then are we conducting an investigation or are we promoting analytical thought?

Brown's new revised schedule of semesters will undoubtedly affect student comprehension, as it will many other areas of our educational process. Members of the faculty will adjust easily, I believe. It seems possible, however, that students will encounter problems completing the work on time. Discussions will become more frantic as those *Dies Irae* between Thanksgiving and Christmas approach. Perhaps we will have to have more lectures and fewer discussion groups as the semester progresses and as fewer assignments are completed, and the semester hurtles towards a close. There will be more mystery about comprehension as the platform rhetoric begins to flow and the minds of students move elsewhere: completion of a term paper long overdue in another course; plane reservations to be picked up for a flight to the West Coast on December 20 (as professors sort out and correct final examinations); storing safely, for the holidays, that most treasured device of collegiate education today, the stereo hi-fi.

With the excellent scores our students present at admission, with the high cost of tuition, with the grand lottery of employment after graduation, *and* with the unlimited talent of our faculty in purveying traditional as well as "new" knowledge, we can understand the desire undergraduates feel for small classes, individual tutorials, and Group Independent Study Projects—all of which run counter to an elaborate program of lecture courses. Even with the many opportunities undergraduates have to hear prominent scholars and figures from public life brought to Brown to lecture, student attendance is in no way as high as it used to be when a Lorimer or a Highet or an Abbé Dimnet would fill Sayles or Alumnae Hall.

Five years ago the call went out from President Swearer for a new capital campaign. Our sentiments were mixed. After all, many of us recollect the hard work that went into the Bicentennial Development Fund, the appeals made to alumni and alumnae at their home base—they had paid off, but the funds came in slowly. Nevertheless people were listening and watching what was happening on College Hill. Now the new call was for $158 million; where could such money be found? We were all very aware of the ill-fated Program for the Seventies, the hoopla in the Corporation Room at its launching, and then its ghostly evaporation with nothing but a postmark to signify its demise. Apparently no one was listening and that at a time when Princeton and Harvard were in the big bucks.

Now, with Howard Swearer's call, apparently our graduates were once more listening. They were reflecting upon the past and they were aware of the future. The Campaign has been a great success, its goal achieved well in advance of the established time limit. Skepticism has yielded to confidence; enthusiastic cooperation appears in all quarters—and at a time of national financial problems. Most impressive has been the designation of funds and gifts. Apparently our graduates did listen attentively in the past, for they have remembered our

Something Old, SOMETHING NEW

Hearts and minds were touched by the philosophical implications of the Campaign for Brown, but the physical plant was affected as dramatically, and much more visibly. The musical sound of construction has been heard all over College Hill the past five years, and it has been a symphonic cacophony that has brought smiles to the faces of crowded geologists and chemists, cramped classical archeologists, underpracticed athletes, and computer scientists yearning to breathe freely.

For our readers who haven't paid the campus a visit recently, we sent illustrator Valerie Marsella out to sketch some of the more tangible results of the successful Campaign.

The Center for Old World Art and Archeology at 70 Waterman was refurbished for $450,000 and opened in October 1981. This building was one of nine departmental houses renovated as part of the Campaign.

e Olney-Margolies Athletic Center sports an ificially surfaced 1.8-acre rooftop named for rner Communciations, Inc.; an advanced heating system that recovers moist heat produced by the Smith Swimming Center; a pricetag of $7 million; and hundreds of satisfied athletes who use it seven days a week, seventeen hours a day.

The Center for Health Care Studies is probably best known to two decades of Brown students as the wind tunnel beneath the Bio-Med Center.

The $2.2-million addition is devoted to Brown's medical students, faculty, and three community-health-oriented programs headquartered at Brown.

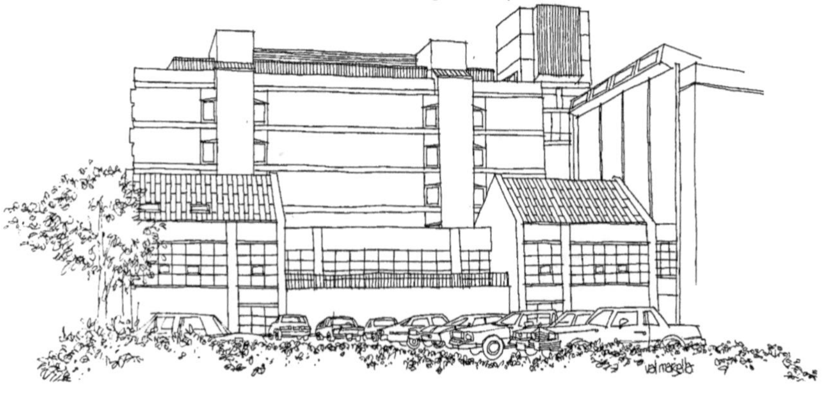

The Geo-Chem building, on the corner of George and Brook Streets, was completed four months ahead of schedule and opened last October. Ironically, only a fraction of the building's $17-million cost has been raised. The five-story building has ninety-six offices and 41,350 square feet of laboratory space.

The addition to the J.W. Wilson Biology Lab is due to be completed this summer, to the tune of $1.6 million.

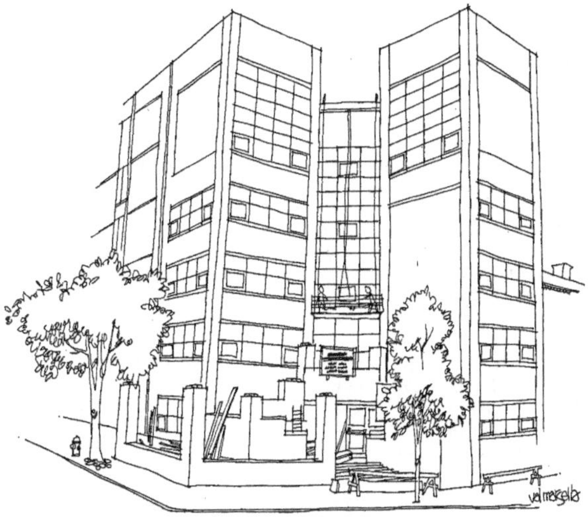

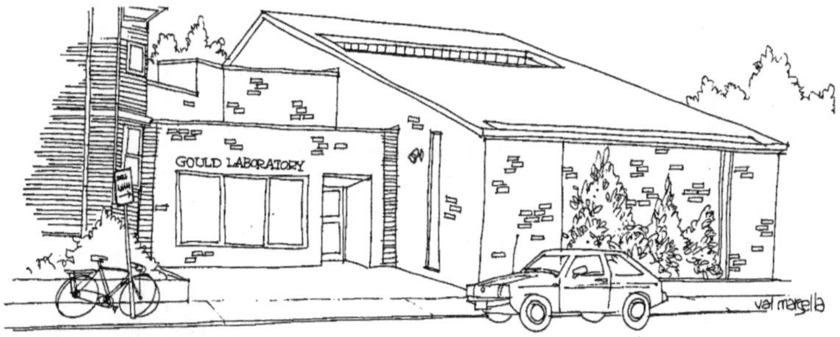

The Gould Laboratory, a wing adjoining the three-story computer science department on Thayer Street, houses the Foxboro Auditorium, a room with sloping tiers of seats and computer workstations—the first learning environment of its kind in the world. The Gould Laboratory, which cost $1 million, was completed in October 1982.

TALK ON PAPER: An Improvised Text on Surfaces and Depths

By Michael Harper

—*memories are old identities*—
(Yeats)

Every shut-eye aint asleep
Every good-bye aint gone
(Folk saying)

First Impressions:

Early January 1970, on a flight from San Francisco to Providence via New York, the proverbial red-eye special; there is snow, the temperature around zero degrees. My uncle, Ernest D. Stokien ('35), had been Phi Beta Kappa at Brown, had been a freshman when Jay Saunders Redding ('28) was a graduate student. Providence was hard to forget: I had done a paper on the Revolutionary War in grade school; Alexander Crummell, free-born and living in Brooklyn in the early nineteenth century, had pastored there—Du Bois had given Crummell an entire chapter in *The Souls of Black Folk,* so profound had been Crummell's commitment and moral struggle with the nation. Frederick Douglass and John Brown had passed through Providence on the Abolitionist trail. I had read Redding's *No Day of Triumph,* an autobiographical travel document written with extraordinary historical resonance and personal style, with particular attention to the Brown days of the '20s; Richard Wright had written an introduction where he made reference to the "Talented Tenth" and one man's search for "truth and understanding."

I stayed in the Biltmore Hotel before the renovation; I was full of the imagery of San Francisco, where I'd lived for almost a decade. The nation was undergoing a periodic reevaluation of its special brand of amnesia, another phase in questioning itself, true from its inception, the Slave Trade, Indians, the *peculiar institution,* a scapegoat set of ideals written out on paper for a few while it improvised itself, while it wrestled with the contradictions of color and democracy, what we say and do. In a few months *Time* would have a special issue on the state of Black America, and Ralph Ellison would write the framing essay "What America Would Be Like Without Blacks."

Ellison says in this important essay:

> Materially, psychologically and culturally, part of the nation's heritage is Negro American, and whatever it becomes will be shaped in part by the Negro's presence. Which is fortunate, for today it is the black American who puts pressure upon the nation to live up to its ideals. It is he who gives creative tension to our struggle for justice and for the elimination of those factors, social and psychological, which make for slums and shabby suburban communities.
>
> It is he who insists that we purify the American language by demanding that there be a closer correlation between the meaning of words and reality, between ideal and conduct, our assertions and our actions. Without the black American, something irrepressibly hopeful and creative would go out of the American spirit, and the nation might well succumb to the moral snobbism that has ever threatened its existence from within. (*Time,* April 6, 1970)

I met Mark Spilka, chairman of English, whom I knew by reputation; it was Saturday, and I was to meet a contingent of black students, and read and comment on my poetry and teaching. I met Charles Philbrick ('44), the poet, whose son (also a poet), Stephen ('71), was a student in Brown's Graduate Writing Program. Redding had stayed with the Philbricks when he visited for one semester in the late 1940s as a guest professor teaching the Negro in American Literature. Now there was another push to integrate in high places, the Ivy League.

'I was sometimes an innocent i

I was always intrigued by the word *integrate*, and with integration. Denotatively it meant whole number; when applied to society it reeked of duplicity, a spectre over race relations and race rituals. The simple answer, a whole number never seemed acceptable as a solution: even *Time* called Ellison's novel *The Invisible Man* when the novel's title was, in actuality, without the article. All across the country, change and amnesia; amputation and gangrene; Roger Williams a zealot and emancipator; the Narragansett Indians nameless, so many living on the fringes, all looking like me.

In my meeting with black students we compared national notes, San Francisco State, Reed College, Oberlin; and we discussed books, including the one I'd had accepted for publication, *Dear John, Dear Coltrane*. (Coltrane was newly dead.) The book had been submitted for a competition, and though it had not won, it had been rescued by Gwendolyn Brooks, one of three judges, who brought it to light. Her name had arisen, now and then, when I was at the Writers Workshop in Iowa; Paul Engle had chosen her poems as a contest winner in suburban Chicago. She was not supposed to win, and Engle had broken another invisible rule.

When I read my poems I marveled at the acoustics and the portraiture on the walls. I talked briefly of Ellison and Yeats, two writers who'd opened the doors of integration, a melding of form of content, the sacred and the profane, the transcendent beauty (and terror) of art and the political reality. During the reading, a man at the back called out that I was an impostor, stealing from musicians, "nothing but a mockingbird," another version of Phyllis Wheatley, two centuries removed, a veiled reference to minstrelsy and stereotyped reduction.

There was dinner at the Schevills, talk of San Francisco, which we shared, why it was time to get out: Dreams had, once again, turned on geography and I was fated: Providence Plantations.

First Courses:

My first year in residence was 1971; I had had a year's leave in Illinois, written another book, been nominated for several awards, taken my family to Ireland to see the landscape of Yeats. My honors seminar in Yeats was taught with the intensity of the elect and the evangelical. We lived off Highway 44 in North Dighton, Massachusetts, on sixteen acres in a 200-year-old house; it looked like Uncle Tom's Cabin. There were cranberries. The neighbors kept their distance. We waited for the birth of our daughter while I taught classes and wrote, memorizing the family names on the street signs, and in the cemetery. I soon found out I was living on an Indian burial mound, that the house had a "borning" room; upstairs and down I could hardly stand up. I thought of the processes of photography, the reverse technical force field of imagery, the unwritten history, the ancestral icons.

I read on the Connecticut and Ohio poetry circuits to raise money for a down payment on a house; my daughter was born on the one free day in a month of readings. She was born in Boston; the doctor was a relative of one of my students at Brown. I wrote and I lived much as an outsider, though I had discovered, fortuitously, a cousin and her husband, Barbara and Lawrence Sykes, whom I'd known from childhood. Artists are here to disturb the peace; teaching, for me, was a conscious process of forming and reforming character, those selves that regenerate in the process of writing, the faith one brings to the task of making; one learns to improvise against opportunities. Love the process. I developed in direct proportion to people and places, the stories and vocabulary they embody, and the irretrievable losses of the polity, and the soul.

read from his fiction. We went over to Sterling Brown's house, as we'd promised in New York; we looked at the books, and we talked about Whitman, Sandburg, Frost, and about Richard Wright and Ellison. I invited Brown to campus for a lecture, "Images and Reality," and a poetry reading in the Crystal Room, the best room on campus for a poetry reading. I remember Gaines and me rushing for the plane from Washington to Providence, for Gaines had a reading at Brown that evening. We rode in first class on that leg of the trip, a gift from the airlines and a Southern white "literate" attendant, and we talked of Sterling Brown. Gaines read from his collection, *Bloodline;* he chose the story, "Just Like a Tree," which took its title from the old spiritual. The story was told in the multiple point of view, eight voices on the subject of an old woman in Louisiana at the center of a push for change in the South. The story was set in the '60s· Gaines, the oldest of twelve children, said he was saved by the library; he said, "I owe the people who raised me, and I'll do my best."

In 1979, Ralph and Fanny Ellison came to campus for an Ellison Festival; there were fine moments throughout the three-day festival—Ellison's address, his remarks when he received the watercolor of his mentor, Inman Page, the first black graduate (1877) of Brown. But what I remember best was Fanny Ellison coming up to me after a performance, again in the Crystal Room, of "Juneteenth," Ellison's sermon on the transformation from Slavery to Freedom. Juneteenth is a southwestern idiomatic reference to June 19, 1865, the last day on the continent in which slaves were freed. She said to me, "Michael, I never thought I'd ever see this." Two ministers, one a black white man, the other a black black man, talking to the congregation and each other, about the magnitude of human endurance that moment represented, and more, that blacks did not have to apologize for being torn from Africa, that they had paid for their passage as Americans in blood. George Bass had selected the actors, the ministers, Walter Stone and Marvin Campbell, who gave voice to Ellison's text. Nathan A. Scott, Jr., gave a lecture/sermon on the subject of the artistry of *Invisible Man*. Dr. Scott's daughter, Leslie ('76), was one of my advanced writing students in poetry, and she, like her father, had the gift of rhetoric and élan. She also knew William Blake.

The Gift of Students:

There have been many, but the one who stands out is Gayl Jones ('73 A.M., '75 D.A.), the novelist, whom William Meredith sent to me from Connecticut College via Lexington, Kentucky. She had little to say in our meetings in independent study, but I sent a box of manuscripts to Toni Morrison, the novelist and editor at Random House. The box weighed twenty-two pounds. Gayl could do anything with form—revise, expand, voice, give texture, provide a mythic design, give her characters a resonant speech akin to the spirituals. One day she gave me a poem, "Deep Song," dedicated to Billie Holiday.

"Deep Song"
from Chant of Saints

The blues calling my name.
She is singing a deep song.
She is singing a deep song.
I am human.
He calls me crazy.
He says, "You must be
crazy."
I say, "Yes, I'm crazy."
He sits with his knees apart.
His fly is broken.
She is singing a deep song.
He smiles.
She is singing a deep song.
"Yes, I'm crazy.
I care about you.
I care.
I care about you.
I care.
He lifts his eyebrows.
The blues is calling my name.
I tell him he'd better
do something about his fly.
He says something softly.
He says something so softly
that I can't even hear him.
He is a dark man.
Sometimes he is a good dark man.
Sometimes he is a bad dark man.
I love him.

Travel Notes:

I was an innocent abroad, and sometimes in my own country. My great-grandfather was an AME (African Methodist Episcopal) bishop, born in Ontario, in 1857; his father was a quartermaster in the British Navy, born in British Guiana (now Guyana); his mother was an Ojibwa (Chippewa)

'Writers are f

princess. They say I was marked to him, with a mole in the same place on the shoulder, and the same lust for wandering, and for seeming lost causes. He, more than anyone else, was responsible for my going to Africa, and particularly to South Africa, where he was a missionary bishop for eight years, from 1908-1916. Here is a letter he wrote in his annual report of the Fourteenth Episcopal District of the AME Church.

Bishop John Albert Johnson served as resident Bishop in South Africa for eight years. During his encumbency Evaton College was established, the Fannie Jackson Coppin Girl's Hall erected, and a large plot of ground secured with a view to erecting a home for aged ministers.

Information of great interest and importance with reference to the status of the South African natives is found in the following letter:

"*Annual Report of the Fourteen Episcopal* District *of the African* Methodist *Episcopal Church. To the President and Members of the Council of* Bishops *of the African* Methodist *Episcopal Church in Annual Session Assembled,* Wilberforce, *Ohio, June, 1913.*

Greetings:

I have the honor to submit the following for your information and consideration: For the past eleven months the country has suffered a severe drought which has destroyed the harvest; killed cattle, sheep, and game in many districts. The poor facilities for transportation in some sections greatly embarrassed the efforts to forward relief in the form of provision. The lack of water was an aggravating form of suffering.

A number of our missionaries could not reach the seat of Conference which met in Bloemfontein, Orange Free State, in the end of November, 1912.

During the past year four of our most efficient elders have died, among them Rev. Henry C. Misikinya, a graduate of Wilberforce University. Two others withdrew under charges, and six were expelled—four natives and two colored—thereby decreasing our ministerial ranks by twelve, a serious loss to our working force.

This lay membership increased several hundred and the financial reports showed an increase over last year.

The attitude of Parliament toward the native and colored residents of the Union is reflected somewhat in the passing of a Bill prohibiting any European from selling or leasing any land to a colored or native person; or any colored or native person selling or leasing any land to a European; restricting travel; and prohibiting a non-resident in a location from remaining over twenty-four hours.

In several cases recently, municipalities have refused a church site to any religious body which does not have a European at its head. Several of our large congregations have been scattered thereby, notably Pretoria and Heidleburg in Transvaal. Pretoria paid over $300 in Dollar Money at the last Conference.

The care of all the churches under such conditions involves much visitation, and the encouragement of much expenditure.

I am earnestly endeavoring to serve our Lord and Church. I do not hesitate to confess my deep sense of need of your prayers for patience and perseverance, and above all, for the grace of God.

I am, my dear brethren,

Your fellow laborer,
J. Albert Johnson
South Africa, March, 1913."

The Honoring of Kin:

Writers, imaginative and critical, are forged in injustice. Some are great liars; they settle on rhetoric and hyperbole, on language as regional idiom and on national stylistics. The shared traditions of the American tongue will not go away. When I should have a split personality, or act as a schizophrenic, I revel in the both/and character of being black and American simultaneously. I have had good teachers, many of them students, who asked the best questions, some still unanswerable.

My best critic, Robert Stepto, influenced his son, Rafael, to provide me my most heartfelt moniker: Michael "Tree." [Professor of English] Elmer Blistein ('42, '53 Ph.D.) gave me his copy of *The Negro Caravan,* edited by Sterling A. Brown, and a copy of [Professor Emeritus of English] I. J. Kapstein's ('26) *Something of a Hero;* [Dean of the College] Harriet Sheridan gave me her

who are driven by brute circumstance to work terribly hard for a living, the living of their families, are very big on formality.

This is what Wright has to say about Mark Twain:

Q. Do you believe that there is such a thing as a good man and a bad man?

Yes. I can read you a passage that defines the bad man about as well as anything I have ever seen. Over in Chapter 15 of *The Adventures of Huckleberry Finn*, Jim and Huck get lost in the fog and are separated from each other. A steamboat goes between them. Huck goes off in the canoe and Jim remains on the raft. Then Huck returns and shows himself to Jim. Jim was so exhausted he had fallen asleep. When he wakes up, he is very glad to see Huck and says "I thought you were dead." Huck pretends that none of this has happened, that Jim has had a dream. Then he asks Jim to interpret the dream in which all these horrible things have happened and Jim gives an elaborate interpretation of it. Then Huck points out that there is some trash, dead leaves and dirt and rocks and so on, stuck on the raft. This proves that all those things really did happen. Huck was just trying to joke with Jim and make fun of him a little bit. Well, here's what Jim does.

> Jim looked at the trash, and then looked at me, and back at the trash again. He had got the dream fixed so strong in his head that he couldn't seem to shake it loose and get the facts back into its place again right away. But when he did get the thing straightened around he looked at me steady without ever smiling, and says:
>
> "What do dey stan' for? I's gwyne to tell you. When I got all wore out wid work, en wid de callin' for you, en went to sleep, my heart wuz mos' broke bekase you wuz los', en I didn' k'yer no' mo' what become er me en de raf'. En when I wake up en fine you back ag'in, all safe en soun', de tears come, en I could' a'got down on my knees en kiss yo foot, I's so thankful. En all you wuz thinkin' 'bout wuz how you could make a fool uv ole Jim wid a lie. Dat truck dah is *trash;* en trash is what people is dat puts dirt on de head er dey fren's en makes 'em ashamed."
>
> Then he got up slow and walked to the wigwam, and went in there without saying anything but that. But that was enough. It made me feel so mean I could almost kissed *his* foot to get him to take it back.
>
> It was fifteen minutes before I could work myself up to go and humble myself to a nigger; but I done it, and I warn't ever sorry for it afterward, neither. I didn't do him no more mean tricks, and I wouldn't done that one if I'd a' knowed it would make him feel that way.

That is a good definition of a bad man.

Hayden said to me, after he'd been at Brown for Commencement, where we'd read together, and he'd received his honorary degree: "This is a special place, Michael, don't you forget it. And don't let the people stop you from writing your poems, like they did me."

When I visited him in Ann Arbor, literally on his deathbed, he made me promise I'd write the poems he couldn't write, not just Matt Henson and Josephine Baker, and his grandson, Michael, but to make the process of composition give up its light: the language needs it and we must work hard to get what it can give.

Stories don't end on deathbeds. He thanked me once more for that student, who'd done an honors thesis on poetry, and gave him the gift of a print of a night-blooming cereus in honor of Hayden and the poem he'd written about the cactus that blooms at midnight, only one bud, its fragrance like the eyes of an enchantress. The students give back something, in an act of transillumination; the student's name was Susan Litwack '76.

I think I'm at the best university I know of; the language tells me so. I do have that *heaviness*, that burden of the weary traveler, and I'm proud. My uncle spent four decades healing the sick without any public notice; he lives in the lives of his patients, as William Carlos Williams lives. Elizabeth Bishop was here; she wrote many memorable poems, one for Billie Holiday. When we were judges together, just before she died, she said, "That was the best poet I ever heard, but what could I do with that music?" And my co-editor, Robert Stepto, gave a brilliant talk here, "Make One Music As Before." Confluences and continuities.

"Who knows but that, on the lower frequencies, I speak for you?"

Michael Harper is the I. J. Kapstein Professor of English.

THE CLASSES

written by Peter Mandel *and* Cynthia Bal

21 "Greetings 1921!" writes *Francis E. Booth*, Stoneham, Mass. "Though I am a diabetic and a double amputee confined to a wheelchair, I am still getting a lot out of life and trying to put some back. I have a driver who takes me for a ride of two hours or more Monday through Friday. Cheers!"

23 *Forrest Paige*, Orange City, Fla., and his wife have sold their home and purchased a condominium at 101 Grande Plaza Dr., Apt. D3, Orange City 32763.

Belmira E. Tavares, Fall River, Mass., received four awards on Fall River's Luso-American Day in February. These included one from *O Jornal*, a Portuguese newspaper, in recognition of her work in the field of education; one from the mayor for her fifty years of service to the school department and the community; one from the Fall River City Council for "her outstanding service to the people of Fall River as a teacher, administrator, and author"; and an Official Citation from the Massachusetts State Senate.

24 *Earle C. Drake*, Syracuse, N.Y., writes: "With the admission this fall of *Tom Drake* to Brown's class of '86, we are five active Brown men." Besides Earle and Tom, there are *E. Clinton Drake* '52, *Henry W. Drake* '58, and *Charles Drake* '58.

In March, the Providence Art Club announced an exhibition that included sculptures in wood, metal, and enamels by *Carleton Goff*.

26 *H. Cushman Anthony*, president of the class, writes: "Our off-year reunion will be especially important as we will be rededicating our 1926 Memorial Park with its additional benches, plantings, and walkways. Set aside Friday, June 3, and join us. We'll gather at our class table under the tent of the all-college reception on the Wriston Quadrangle. The cash bar is open at 5 o'clock, and while we are still under control, we will venture over to our little park where you can try out our new benches and witness the presentation to the University of our payment in full."

27 *Elizabeth Armstrong Bucholz* and *Theta Holmes Wolf*, Hollywood, Fla., were unable to attend their 55th reunion, so they had one of their own when they met to attend the Brown banquet held at the Flagler Museum in Palm Beach on March 17. "'27 seemed to be the oldest class represented, except for a gentleman from the class of '19."

George P. Richardson, Jr., Fairfax, Calif., reports that he will be enjoying a free cruise from Miami to Acapulco on the *Royal Odyssey*. He'll be one of 150 hosts to 300 women, and "all guys and gals will be legally single. The gals pay!" he writes. "It's a big promotion for ex-Navy officers and 'gentlemen only."

29 *David Aldrich*, Providence, R.I., exhibited watercolor landscapes at the Providence Art Club in March.

Robert P. Montague, Southbridge, Mass., recently celebrated a dual anniversary. In November 1982, a dinner was held in honor of his having reached the age of 75 and passed the fifty-year mark as a member of the Massachusetts Bar. Bob is the senior partner in the law firm of Montague and Desautels in Southbridge.

30 *Winthrop Southworth*, Chevy Chase, Md., has ended his service on a United Nations committee reviewing the administrative statutes of the organization He is now completely retired and is "savoring life in Chevy Chase."

31 *Bill Schofield*, Newton, Mass., ha been selected for biographical lis ing in the 1982-83 edition of *Who's Who in the World*. Bill is a retired Navy captain an a former Boston journalist and foreign cor respondent.

Jane Reid Tait, Kerrville, Texas, writes that she is now retired. Her husband, Rob ert, died in 1981.

33 *Violet Bander Callahan* is traveling from her home in Hawaii for the reunion, stopping on the way to see her s in Aurora, Colorado, and spending the week before the reunion with *Rae Baldwin Scattergood*.

Ruth Wade Cerjanec, secretary of the Pembroke class, writes: "We are looking forward to the biggest gathering of our cla since June 1933. Class members are comin from all over the country to renew old friendships."

Frances B. Cowell, Warwick, R.I., has r tired from teaching in the Warwick public schools.

Dr. *John R. Ewan*, Washington, D.C., sends word that he is still in active practice of medicine. "I began in D.C. in 1943," he writes. "*Tempus Fugit!*"

J. Morton Ferrier, Jr., Santa Fe, N.M., reports: "My daughter Isabelle Moya's horse, 'Star,' was just that—it won third place in the World Quarter Horse Champi onship Show at Oklahoma City."

Mildred Sullivan Gavagan, South Dartmouth, Mass., keeps busy with her grand children. Her daughter, Francine, married son of *Josh Weeks* '19, who was a member the Brown football team that went to the first Rose Bowl game in 1916.

Jean Bauer Glantz, Albuquerque, N.M. has a new granddaughter, born to her so Richard. Her daughter, Martha, has a son and a daughter.

Edward Kreisler, Madrid, Spain, receiv The Cross of Isabel The Catholic from Kin Juan Carlos of Spain in November 1981. This is considered Spain's highest honor. Edward founded and is president of Kreis ler's Galerias, a collection of "exclusively Spanish" crafts, gifts, and art. He is hopi

Republic of Panama to find life in the heart of Dixie pleasant and affordable in retirement. I'm planning to attend the 45th and 50th reunions, after being out of touch for forty years."

40 *Harry B. Henshel*, Flushing, N.Y., recently was elected vice chairman of the board of trustees of Adelphi University. He has served on the board since 1955.

Roy Hunt is a vice president of Spencer Stuart and Associates, an executive search consulting firm in New York City. His son, *Donald Hunt* '73, has joined a competitor, Arthur Young and Company, four blocks south on Park Avenue.

41 Dr. *Allen R. Ferguson*, Washington, D.C., is president of the Public Interest Economics Foundation. He writes that the foundation has recently established the National Institute of Economics and Law, "which is lobbying against various attempts to weaken antitrust laws in such areas as ocean shipping, medical practice, and exclusive territorial franchises. "Brown economics professor George Borts is a member of the foundation's Board of Economic Advisers.

Dr. *William E. Fraser*, Dunedin, Fla., reports the birth of his grandson, Ian Matthew Fraser, on Oct. 22, 1982.

Capt. *Arthur A. Helgerson*, Lexington Park, Md., retired from the Navy Medical Corps in 1978, after thirty-two years of service. "Gardening and genealogy are my retirement activities," he writes.

George Hurley, Jr., Silver Spring, Md., and his wife were recently in Seattle where they "house-sat" for their son and daughter-in-law and visited *Steve Stone's* Capt. Whidbey's Inn.

George McTammany, Foxboro, Mass., reports that he retired last year "after thirty-five years of service with the Foxboro Company." He had been in purchasing.

42 Dr. *Irving J. Casey*, Schenectady, N.Y., retired last May from Russell Sage College. He had been professor of sociology and chairman of the department of sociology and anthropology.

A. Wilber Stevens, Las Vegas, Nev., sends word to his classmates that he continues as professor of humanities at the University of Nevada at Las Vegas. He is "leading a second life" as theatre and music critic for the *Las Vegas Sun*, and was married on Feb. 12 to Loucinda Wilder Davis.

43 *Arlene Rome Ten Eyck*, secretary for the Pembroke class, writes: "Proof that life begins at forty is almost here. Your reunion committee met on Feb. 28 to finalize plans for this once-in-a-lifetime event. We have included in our 'menu' a musical cabaret at Leeds Theatre, dinner at the Graduate Center, musicale at the Grant Recital Hall, and a clambake at ye old Fieldhouse. Your attendance will make this our best reunion ever."

Stanley W. Allen, Fairhaven, Mass., reports that he has retired as a vice president of INA Reinsurance Company in Philadelphia. He and his wife are building a new home at 18 Bent Tree Ln., Hilton Head Plantation, Hilton Head Island, S.C. 29928.

John G. Confrey, Riverside, Conn., writes that he has retired as vice president and manager of the Midtown West office of Chubb and Son, Inc., in New York City.

1982 was "a very exciting year" for *Bernice Parvey Solish* and her family. "In July," she writes, "our oldest son, Alfred, and his wife, Peg, presented us with our first grandchild, Benjamin Seth. Alfred is in his last year of training in ophthalmology at the Jules Stein Institute at UCLA. His wife is an astrophysicist at the Jet Propulsion Laboratories in Pasadena. On Oct. 2, our daughter, Sharyn, married Dr. Michael Siegel, who is in his final year of a residency in neurology at Mount Sinai Hospital in New York. *Samuel* '79, our youngest, helped round out the joyous year by announcing his engagement on Oct. 19 to *Martha Smith* '79. Sam is a student at Tufts Medical School in Boston, and Muffie, who received her M.P.H. and M.B.A. at Columbia, works as a medical management consultant at Amherst Associates in Amherst, Mass."

44

Dr. *Hermes C. Grillo*, Boston, Mass., reports that he is still serving as chief of thoracic surgery at Massachusetts General Hospital. His daughter, *Amy* '86, is now at Brown.

45

Hawley O. Judd, Eastham, Mass., retired from The Travelers Insurance Company in 1980 as second vice president. In January, he moved to Eastham from Connecticut.

Nancy Page, Savannah, Ga., had a book, *Bobby Orr*, published in November. It's part of the Dell Laurel Leaf juvenile series.

46

Alice Clark Donahue, Barrington, R.I., served as co-chairman of the 1983 United Cerebral Palsy telethon. She is past president and an honorary member of the Junior Women's Club of Barrington.

Robert W. Jahn, Hobe Sound, Fla., writes: "I've been appointed national chairman of the Fifty-Plus Committee for NAHB. I'm currently developing 'Eaglewood'— a fifty-plus community in Hobe Sound."

Barbara Martin Leonard, Providence, received the 1983 Honor Award from the National Jewish Hospital/National Asthma Center. She is chairman of the board and treasurer of H and H Screw Products Manufacturing Company in Ashton, R.I., and is a Brown trustee.

Allen Rust, Orange Park, Fla., took a motorcycle trip last June from Florida to Massachusetts in order to visit his sister, *Judy* '48, and her husband, *John Ellington* '49. "I've also visited *Bob O'Donoghue* '46 outside of Ocala, Fla., where he and his wife operate a citrus grove."

48

Class Reporter *Christine Dunlap Farnham* writes: "There's still time to make your reservations for the fabulous 35th commencement weekend. Send in your reservation form now, or telephone *Nancy Cantor Eddy* at (617) 872-9656 or *Betty Montali Smith* at (617) 222-2718 for further information. Contributions to the Class of 1948 Scholarship Fund are still welcome. We still need more to reach the $25,000 goal for the fund. Checks can be made payable to Brown University and enclosed with your reservation form, or sent directly to the Brown Fund, Box 1893, Brown University."

Robert C. Barnes and *George T. LaBonne* '49 are both members of the executive committee of the Manchester Community College Foundation, which has established the Manchester (N.H.) Regional Arts Center, Inc., to raise funds to build and operate a performing arts center for the region. Bob is president of the new corporation, Ted is its treasurer, and both are on its executive board.

49

Arthur Bobrick, New York City, has joined the New York sales staff of *Life* magazine. Previously, he had been publisher of *Intellectual Digest* and an advertising salesman for *Psychology Today*.

Theodore A. Hirt, Warren, Ohio, reports that he has retired after thirty-three years with the Thomas Steel Strip Corporation. He has become a private consultant in the field of continuous strip electroplating.

50

Lester R. Allen, Jr., Simsbury, Conn., has opened a firm called A and D Communicators, which will "rent public relations executive time by the day, week, or month to help businesses plan and conduct information projects." He also reports the birth of his first grandchild, Lester R. Allen IV, in Yarmouth, Mass..

Maurice A. Bissonnette, Providence, has been elected senior resident officer and associate director of the Tucker, Anthony and R.L. Day securities firm. He had been serving as vice president with the company.

Janice Peterson Michael, Wynnewood, Pa., reports the birth of her granddaughter, Catherine Meehan Rogers, in December.

Dr. *William E. Parker*, Laguna Hills, Calif., is president of Statek Corporation, a manufacturer of quartz crystals used for frequency control. The Parker family is now spread coast to coast with *William E. Parker II* '70 in Bristol, R.I., *Robert N. Parker* '76 at Rutgers in New Brunswick, N.J., and Nancy J. Parker, a marine, at Camp Pendleton, Calif.

51

Nancy Welch Dalton sends word that all three of her sons have graduated from the College of William and Mary, and that "all three were Kappa Sigma. Keith is working for Steve, who has a chain of appliance-parts stores in the Maryland-Delaware area. Brian has just been promoted to treasurer of Fiduciary Trust in Dallas." She is "especially proud" of her uncle, *Paul Welch* '38, who was elected to Brown's Hall of Fame in baseball.

Harvey B. Sindle, New York, N.Y., continnes his entertainment, literary property, and copyright law practice at 400 Madison Ave. "My experiences as an undergraduate member of the Brown Band and WBRU have proved quite helpful," he says.

Robert L. Warsh, Loudonville, N.Y., writes: "I have sold our group of Little Folks stores that were based in Albany, N.Y., to the U.S. Shoe Corporation. We have established new executive offices and a distribution center in Albany, and I will stay with the corporation as president and CEO of the children's wear division."

Fla. The Florida Bach Festival is the second oldest continuing festival of its kind in the U.S.

Dr. *Emil Soucar*, Wenonah, N.J., is director of the family therapy clinic in the department of counseling psychology at Temple University in Philadelphia. He has recently opened a private practice in Pitman, N.J.

David Wilson and *Susan Tollefson Wilson* '61, East Greenwich, R.I., write: "We are proud to have our daughter, *Nancy*, in the Brown class of '86!"

59

Col. *Richard J. Beland* is director of safety for the U.S. Air Force in Europe. He's stationed at Ramstein Air Force Base in Germany, where his boss is Brig. Gen. *Bob Norman* '57.

Donna Lewiss Brock, Huntsville, Ala., is an engineer with the U.S. Army Missile Command and has been selected for the Army Materiel Acquisition and Readiness Executive Development Program. She writes: "I have two children, Mark and Michelle, who attend the Randolph School in Huntsville. Last year, I was president of the Mason-Dixon Toastmasters Club, which was named one of the top ten clubs of the world."

The *Denver Post* writes that *Lew Cady*, Denver, Colo., was the organizer of a massive "pub crawl" on Denver's Colfax Avenue. "Cady is a beverage consumer of note," says the *Post*, "and a member of Bar Tourists of America—a nationwide organization of men and women with time on their hands."

John H. Hickman, Geneseo, N.Y., has been elected to the board of directors of National Health Care, Inc., a nursing-home chain with facilities in New York, Connecticut, and Florida.

W. Thomas Knight, Haworth, N.J., has been named group vice president-general counsel and secretary of Avon Products, Inc. His responsibilities will include both United States and international legal affairs and public affairs.

Aaron Seidman, Brookline, Mass., is designing computer graphics data analysis programs for Digital Equipment Corporation. "I discovered I was a latent computer freak," he says. His wife is *Ruth Kertzer Seidman* (see '60).

Jean Sheridan, Wickford, R.I., commutes to Providence College, where she is acquisition librarian. "My four children, Sue, Mark, Julie, and Liz, are scattering. Sue graduated from St. Lawrence last May, Mark is at URI, Julie enters Emerson in the fall, and Liz is the only girl trumpet player in the North Kingstown High School band."

60

Rebekah Hill Eckstein's M.A. student exhibition was held in April at the Courtney Gallery of Jersey City State College. She has two sons.

Martha Hoyt Kinsella, Oxford, Mich., is producing programs for cable television, "including a local news program, an aerobic exercise show, real estate hints, and wholesome foods interviews." She adds: "It's not quite like classmate *Ted Turner*, but in the same ballgame." Before her TV work, she had spent eight years with newspapers in New Haven, London, and the Detroit area, and five years as a public information coordinator with an Oakland County (Michigan) human service agency.

Ruth Kertzer Seidman has been appointed director of the research library at the Air Force Geophysics Laboratory, Hanscom Air Force Base, in Bedford, Mass. She is immediate past president of the Boston chapter of the Special Libraries Association. Her husband is *Aaron Seidman* (see '59).

61

Elizabeth Diggs, New York City, is one of five winning playwrights in the Foundation of The Dramatists Guild/CBS New Plays Contest. Her winning play, *Goodbye Freddy*, is being presented this spring at the South Coast Repertory in Costa Mesa, Calif. She writes: "I left academic life (teaching literature and writing) to write plays full time, and I'm delighted to be surviving at it. My first play, *Close Ties*, will be produced in England this summer at Alan Ayckbourn's Stephen Joseph Theatre in the Round in Scarborough. I'm now at work on a new play, *R.J.'s War*, commissioned by South Coast Repertory. I've written a screenplay of my one-act play, *Dumping Ground*, which is scheduled for production soon." She writes that her daughter, *Jennifer Mackenzie*, is a junior at Brown, and her niece, *Alexandra Maytag*, is a freshman. "Of course, they both love it." Alexandra is the daughter of Elizabeth's sister, *Lucy Diggs* '63. Elizabeth's new address is 219 Mulberry St., New York 10012. She also recently bought a 1795 farmhouse in Chatham, N.Y.

Lewis L. Gould, Austin, Texas, chairman of the history department of the University of Texas, gave a new course last fall on "First Ladies in the 20th Century." His book, *The Spanish American War and President McKinley*, was recently published in paperback by the University Press of Kansas.

David Meister, New York City, has been appointed senior vice president of Home Box Office Enterprises in New York City. Among his duties will be the responsibility for all Cinemax programming and HBO family programming.

James C. Murray, Rosemead, Calif., reports that he is a senior financial management information systems analyst for Interstate Electronics Corporation in Anaheim, Calif. "I design and implement manual and automated financial applications on mainframe computers." He and his wife, Judy, have two sons, David, 17, and Paul, 14.

George M. Nebel, Suffern, N.Y., reports that he is a major in the Marine Reserves and a district manager for the New York Telephone Company. He and his wife, Joan, have two sons, Marty and Ricky.

Juliana Thacher Plummer, New York City, is director of youth employment programs for the New York City Mission Society—"the oldest social service agency in New York."

Douglas R. Riggs was married on Oct. 16 to Mary Mills of Newport, R.I., where they are living. The ushers included *Anthony L. DiBiasio* '77. Doug, a feature writer for the *Providence Sunday Journal*, is the son of Professor Emeritus Lorrin A. Riggs, who retired five years ago as the L. Herbert Ballou Professor of Psychology at Brown.

Edward D. Rotmer, Cranston, R.I., reports that his daughter, Michelle, is a prelaw student at Rutgers.

W. Peter Teagan, Acton, Mass., recently headed up an energy task force in Pakistan for the U.S. Agency for International Development. Peter is a senior consultant with Arthur D. Little, Inc., in Cambridge, Mass..

62 *Stephen Joseph*, Boston, is now an associate professor of philosophy at Framingham State College in Framingham, Mass..

Thomas H. Wilson, Houston, will lead the 1983 campaign of the United Way of the Texas Gulf Coast. He is chairman of the board and chief executive officer of Capital Bank West Loop.

63 *Richard M. Bernstein*, Wynnewood, Pa., and his wife, Christine M. Wilson (Wellesley '72), report the birth of their first child, David Paul, on Aug. 15.

Carole Jones Dineen, New York City, has been appointed fiscal assistant secretary at the Department of the Treasury. She will oversee Treasury's management of the government's financial operations, cash management for the government, raising money to finance government debt, directing the performance of the fiscal agency functions of the Federal Reserve Banks, and handling the investments of the multi-billion-dollar trust and other accounts of the U.S. government. She had been a vice president of Bankers Trust Company in New York City.

Nancy Frazier Herman, Cooperstown, N.Y., writes: "My son, *Peter B. Freehafer*, is a member of the class of '86. Susie is a junior at St. Paul's School, and Lisa is 13 and at home at Cooperstown."

C. Martin Lawyer, Tampa, Fla., writes that he is "still serving on the front line in the war on poverty" as staff attorney for Bay Area Legal Services. "Last April," he reports, "I anchored the defense as 'sweeper' for the lawyers' soccer team in its annual match against the doctors, which ended in a draw, and won my age group in the lawyer-doctor five-kilometer race, placing fifth overall."

Dr. *John H. Mensher*, Seattle, Wash., sends word that he is "very happy in the Pacific Northwest" after spending twelve years at the University of Iowa. John is a partner at the Mason Clinic (section of ophthalmology). He's married and has two sons, Daniel, 7, and Ian, 3.

Carol Burchard O'Hare, Cambridge, Mass., has recently become assistant general counsel for Boston University. Prior to this, she had been an associate with a Boston law firm and a teacher of visually-handicapped public school students for a group of Massachusetts communities.

William C. Schnell, Huntington, N.Y., has recently retired from his aerospace engineering career at Grumman Aerospace Corporation in order to devote more time to three corporations he owns: Family Aids, Inc., a home health care organization; Mechtron Industries, a manufacturing concern; and Uniforms Unlimited, a retail outlet.

Jon Zeder, Miami, Fla., reports the birth of his second son, Evan, on Nov. 19.

64 *Yolanda Maione Bernardini*, Rome, Italy, and her husband have moved from Paris to Rome and plan to settle there indefinitely. Their children, Guilia, 13, and G.B., 10, attend the American Overseas School of Rome and are "enjoying the best of two worlds."

Patrick Fleury, Plattsburgh, N.Y., has been promoted to professor at the State University of New York College at Plattsburgh. He joined the mathematics department at the college in 1970, after two years as a lecturer at McGill University.

Michael Lee Gradison, Indianapolis, has been appointed executive director of the Indiana affiliate of the American Civil Liberties Union. "In addition, I have begun my fourth term as president of the Indiana Repertory Theatre here in Indianapolis."

James R. Johnson and Lee Shepard, of Weston, Mass, were married on June 5 in Wellesley. Ushers were *Robert Adams* '63, *Gerald Johnson* '69, and *H. Gary Uphouse* '67. After fifteen years with Westinghouse, Jim is now president of Merit Liquors in Medford, Mass.

Peter T. LeClair, Wayne, Pa., has joined Philadelphia Life Insurance Company as senior vice president and chief actuary. He is a fellow of the Society of Actuaries, a member of the American Academy of Actuaries, a Chartered Life Underwriter, and a fellow of the Life Management Institute. He, his wife, Donna, and their three daughters now live at 9 Academy Ln., Wayne 19087.

Barbara Zwick Lewin, Chesterfield, Mo., writes: "I am now working as a social worker in industry, setting up employee motivation programs. My husband, David, owns a bookbinding business; our daughter, Cindy, is 13, and son, Brad, is 12."

Conrad Ober, Eugene, Oreg., and his wife, Elaine, report the birth of their third child, Andrew Lyle Ober. Conrad is "program director for a sheltered workshop in Eugene."

Charles B. Weinberg, Vancouver, B.C., is professor and chairman of the Division of Marketing in the Faculty of Commerce and Business Administration, University of British Columbia. His book, *Marketing for Public and Nonprofit Managers*, will be published by John Wiley and Sons this spring. His wife is *Joanne Blumenfeld Weinberg* (see '65). They have two daughters, Beth, 13, and Amy, 8.

Francis D. Wright, Annapolis, Md., and his wife, Gayle, announce the arrival of their second child, Elizabeth Williams, last Aug. 18. Fran is now controller of the Edward A. Myerberg Company, a Baltimore real estate developer and property management company.

65 *Peter R. Newsted*, Calgary, Alberta, and his wife have recently returned from a year's sabbatical in England, where Pete was working at the University of Leeds in Yorkshire. He is an associate professor and academic director of computing for the Faculty of Management at the University of Calgary in Calgary, Alberta.

Lawrence M. Silverman, Plymouth, Mass., continues as rabbi of Congregation Beth Jacob in Plymouth. On Nov. 7, he ran in the 1982 Ocean State Marathon in Newport, R.I.

Joanne Blumenfeld Weinberg, Vancouver, B.C., was appointed assistant professor of anatomy, School of Medicine, University of British Columbia, last July. She received a British Columbia Health Care Research Foundation Scholarship and is pursuing re-

Merrill. Gwyneth's *Fanfare*, *Interlude*, and *Finale* were premiered by the Twin Cities Symphony in February, and her *Second Piano Sonata* was performed by pianist Michael Haberkörn at the Lincoln Center Library last November.

Jeffrey L. Walters, Ann Arbor, Mich., has joined a family business that manufactures architectural doors and components for office furniture. "We have a plant in Michigan and will be opening another in Florida this spring."

John M. Walcott has established a new firm, Walcott Systems and Associates, to provide consulting and programming services to users of IBM computer systems.

69

Barbara Bertsch Boyd, Fort Washington, Md., reports that she is currently program manager of the Senior Executive Service Candidate Development Program for the U.S. Department of Health and Human Services. Her husband, John, is a psychological counselor and family therapist with the Alexandria (Va.) Division of Mental Health, Mental Retardation, and Substance Abuse.

Chris Coles was the production manager on one of the short films nominated in this year's Oscars. *Ballet Robotique*, nominated for Best Live Action Short Subject, was a departure for Chris, who usually works on full-length films such as *The Jazz Singer*, *Superman*, and currently, *Supergirl*.

Robin Winkler Doroshow, Upland, Calif., and her husband, Dr. James Doroshow, report the birth of their first child, Deborah Blythe, on Feb. 7.

Gilbert N. Lewis was married on July 3, 1982, to Susan T. Bagley. He also received a promotion to associate professor of mathematics at Michigan Technological University. They live in Houghton, Mich.

Thomas K. Lindsey, Lubbock, Texas, has been promoted to captain in the U.S. Army Reserve.

Barbara Gershon Ryder, Metuchen, N.J., completed her doctorate in computer science at Rutgers University last August. She is now an assistant professor there. She and her husband, Jonathan, have two children, Beth Ann and Andrew.

Andrew Stanhope and Nancy Sweeney, of Spring Lake, N.J., were married recently and are living in Barrington, R.I. He is manager of financial planning for a subsidiary of W.R. Grace & Company.

Terry Warburton, Golden, Colo., writes: "As I should have expected, fourteen years passed before enough happened in my life so that I had something to submit for the class notes. Janice E. Salomon and I were married in Golden, Colo., in 1980. Janice is on leave from her position at National Jewish Hospital while she cares for our daughter, Jaime Sarah, who was born on September 23, 1982. I am a teaching fellow and a doctoral candidate in the speech communication department of the University of Denver; that lets me watch my students leave for weekends of skiing while I grade papers and help Janice change diapers. I have also been a regular commentator on the local National Public Radio affiliate, talking about the lunacy of public figures and issues. (Obviously, material is not hard to find.)"

John F. Wilkinson, Jr., and his wife, *Jenny Littlepage Wilkinson* (see '71), Columbia, Md., report the birth of their third child, Evan, on Dec. 27. John is a personnel officer with the Department of the Interior.

70

Norine Duncan Cashman and her husband, *David*, of Providence, report that their daughter, Eleanor, is 5 years old. Norine, who is curator of slides and photographs in Brown's art department, is a participant in the 1982-83 management development program at the University. David is in his fifth year of teaching English at Providence Country Day School.

David M. Fox and Annette Susan Benda were married on June 20. They are living in New York City. *Edward S. Katz* '71 was best man. Annette graduated from Queens College, summa cum laude and Phi Beta Kappa, in 1971.

Joy Javits, Chapel Hill, N.C., is a teacher and choreographer. She returned to Brown recently to choreograph a movement piece, "Friendship 1st," for the Dance Extension. "They danced, moved, spoke, and wrote their own part of it. [Lecturer in Theatre Arts] Julie Strandberg is a wonderful lady." Joy and her husband, David Romero, are going to be moving to Los Angeles in the fall. "Anybody have a place for us to move into?" She writes that she enjoyed being back at Brown. "The students and faculty are intelligent and kind, and I remembered the good years I had spent there in 1966-70."

Janice B. Kruger, Washington, D.C., graduated from Franklin Pierce Law Center in May and passed her D.C. bar exam. She is working for the International Human Rights Law Group in Washington.

71

Dr. *Patricia L. Gerbarg* and her husband, Dr. Nelson M. Braslow, of Newton Highlands, Mass., report the birth of their son, Joshua Ross Braslow, on May 13, 1982.

James A. Hochman and Linda Legner were married on Sept. 5 in Chicago, where they are living. Linda is president of the Legner Group, Inc., a marketing communications firm.

Meredith Roosa Inderfurth and her husband, Rick, of Arlington, Va., report the birth of their daughter, Ashley Ann, on Feb. 18, 1982.

William R. Leigh, Holliston, Mass., is a manager of language development at Software Arts, Inc., located at 27 Mica Ln., Wellesley, Mass. 02181.

James L. Nolan and Armina Sheets were married Oct. 9 in Kent, Wash. They are living in Seattle, with their 3-year-old son, Matthew. Both James and Armina are employed by the Puget Sound Air Pollution Control Agency.

Howard E. Peskoe, Glen Rock, N.J., has become a member of the New York City law firm of Cole & Dietz. His appointment was effective Feb. 1.

Dan Riesenberg and his wife, Laura, of San Diego, report the birth of their second child, David, on Dec. 17. Their first son, John, is 3. Dan is an attorney with the law firm of Luce, Forward, Hamilton & Scripps, specializing in the law relating to employee benefits.

Paul Schopf, Hyattsville, Md., is a research oceanographer with NASA at the Goddard Space Flight Center. His wife is *Jane Seigler* (see '73).

Ruby Shang, New York City, a dancer and choreographer, is the U.S. Steel Foundation Affiliate Artist for this coming year Ruby has performed throughout the U.S., Canada, Europe, the People's Republic of China, and Japan. She recently received a Fulbright grant to choreograph and perform in New Zealand. Ruby spent the years 1971-75 with the Paul Taylor Dance Company.

Dr. *Dan Small* ('75 M.D., '73 M.M.Sc.), his wife, Jan, and son, Evan, are living in San Luis Obispo, Calif. Dan is practicing rheumatology, immunology, and internal medicine at the San Luis Medical Clinic.

Dr. *David A. Snyder*, Boca Raton, Fla., is in the private practice of ophthalmology in Delray Beach and Boca Raton. He and his wife, Marsha, have two sons, Jeffrey, 3, and Eric, 1.

Dr. *Barry Stults*, Salt Lake City, Utah, is an assistant professor of medicine at the University of Utah Medical Center. His wife, Connie, is also a physician. They have a 2-year-old daughter, Cheryl.

Jenny Littlepage Wilkinson and her husband, *John F. Wilkinson* (see '69), report the birth of their third child, Evan Littlepage Wilkinson. Jenny is an adoptions social worker, under contract with Lutheran Social Services.

Daryl Dodson Wilson and her husband, Wallace, report the birth of their daughter, Connery Amelia Wilson, on Nov. 3.

72 *George H. Billings*, Arlington, Va., has been promoted from vice president, business development, of Satellite Television Corporation, the direct broadcast satellite of COMSAT, to vice president, corporate development, of the parent company, with responsibility for corporate strategy, mergers, and acquisitions.

Dr. *Reid W. Coleman* ('75 M.D) and his wife, Kate, report the birth of their second child, Laura Jeanne, on Sept. 22.

W. Hudson Connery and his wife, Cathy, of Coral Springs, Fla., report the birth of their son, William Hudson Connery III, on Oct. 25.

Dr. *William C. Graham* ('75 M.D.), Huntington, W.Va., is assistant professor of medicine in the section of infectious diseases at Marshall University School of Medicine. The school graduated its first class in 1981.

Douglas A. Price, Tampa, Fla., will be graduating in June from Life Chiropractic College. He specializes in sports injuries and lower back pain. He is competing in body building, having won the Mr. Dixie, Mr. Peach State, and many other titles.

Leonard Schlesinger, Arlington, Mass., has been promoted to associate professor of organizational behavior/human resource management at Harvard Business School. He is the author of the recently-published *Quality of Worklife and the Supervisor* (Praeger) and *Managing Behavior in Organizations* (McGraw-Hill). A forthcoming book is entitled *Recasting Bell: From Monopoly to Competition at AT&T* (Scott Foresman). His wife is *Phyllis Fineman Schlesinger* (see '73).

Michael T. Schmutte, Bay Village, Ohio, received his chartered life casualty underwriter designation at the national CPCU convention in Miami Beach in October.

Moe Shore, Cambridge, Mass., has a video company called "Show More Video" in Cambridge. He also recently edited a Nova program for public television.

Adolph E. Vezza and Denise Marie Walker were married on July 17, 1981. They are living in Gallup, N.M., where they are practicing registered pharmacists.

Frederick Wang, Lincoln, Mass., has been named executive vice president and chief development officer at Wang Laboratories in Lowell, Mass. He had been senior vice president, development.

David R. Weaver, Los Angeles, has been appointed an assistant professor of architecture in the School of Environmental Design, California State Polytechnic University, Pomona, Calif.

Ben Wiles has moved from New York City to Albany, where he is assistant counsel to Gov. Mario Cuomo.

73 *Nan Chalat*, Oakley, Utah, writes: "Never meant to stay so long in Utah, but it is an awesomely beautiful state. I am a freelance photojournalist, which never provides any financial security, but the freedom is wonderful. If friends find themselves skiing in Park City, I can be contacted through the newspaper there."

Alan R. Gallotta and his wife, Dianne, of Braintree, Mass., report the birth of their first child, Leanne Marie, on May 20. Alan is director of athletics and is a computer science teacher at Archbishop Williams High School, Braintree.

Raymond F. Gorman and Helen Louise Craig were married on Jan. 8. They are living in College Park, Md., where Raymond is an assistant professor of finance at the University of Maryland. He completed his doctor of business administration degree from Indiana University last May.

Mary E. Griffin, Washington, D.C., is an architect with Hartman-Cox in Washington.

Dr. *Jeff Harper*, Houston, is an assistant professor of endocrinology at the University of Texas Medical School. He and his wife, Mary, have a daughter, Katie, 3, and a son, Andrew, 1.

Donald R. Hunt, South Salem, N.Y., is with Arthur Young & Company, New York City, as an executive search consultant.

Kevin "Floyd" Jaros, Minnetonka, Minn., has been appointed marketing director for new cereals in the Big "G" division of General Mills. Floyd joined the company in 1976 as a marketing assistant and was product manager for Nature Valley Granola Bars, Granola Clusters, and Chewy Granola Bars prior to his new appointment.

Chris Kunzi and his wife, Kathy, of Laguna Niguel, Calif., report the birth of their third child, Taylor Michael Kunzi, on Dec. 15. Their other children are Ryan, 2, and Kimberly, 12.

Thomas Mallon, Stewart Manor, N.Y., is an assistant professor of English at Vassar College and is a frequent contributor to the *National Review*. He spent a sabbatical this year as a visiting scholar at Cambridge University.

Bob Pangia and his wife, Stephanie, of Scotch Plains, N.J., report the birth of their first child, Robert William, Jr., on Sept. 24.

75 *James A. Barker, Jr.*, is a first-year student at the University of Virginia School of Law. "I'm one of the older ones, though far from the oldest, at age 29." His address is 118 Ivy Dr., #7, Charlottesville, Va. 22901.

Geoffrey F. Bowers, New York City, is an associate at the New York City law firm of Phillips, Nizer, Benjamin, Krim & Ballon. He was admitted as an attorney-at-law in New York State, First Judicial Department, in February, and graduated from Yeshiva University's Benjamin N. Cardozo School of Law last June.

William Buffum, Providence, is a forester with the Pan American Development Foundation. He participated in PADF's Agroforestry Extension Project in Haiti, in which citizens of Haiti were encouraged to plant and maintain fast-growing tree seedlings to be harvested in three to five years, thus supplementing the Haitians' income and supporting the goal of reforestation and soil conservation there.

John Fraser and his wife, Claudia, of Dunedin, Fla., are parents of a son, Ian Matthew, born on Oct. 22, according to John's father, Dr. *William E. Fraser* '41.

Geoffrey Garth, Long Beach, Calif., writes: "I weathered my first year as president, shipping clerk, etc., of California Medical Products. We manufacture and market Stifneck, a new type of neck brace that I developed. Working for myself is as much fun as toy designing, my last straight job, and the pay is a lot better. No wife or kids to report. However, my family has grown to include Buzzby, who is half Black Labrador and half Irish Wolfhound, and is now 1 year old."

Dr. *Harold K. Gever* ('78 M.D) and Diana Lynne Turek (Cornell '75) were married on June 14, 1981. They are living in Ventnor, N.J.

Dr. *Christine Gleason*, San Francisco, Calif., has finished her pediatric residency at Case Western Reserve University Hospital in Cleveland, Ohio, and has begun a neonatology fellowship in San Francisco. "I have become an avid squash player and still play the clarinet when I'm inspired."

Brad Hessel, New York City, writes: "Am I the first member of the class of '75 to lose $50,000? (The first and last, I hope). After I'd worked my way up from receptionist to vice president and 10-percent owner, the publishing company I had been at since August 1975 slid under the waves last spring—just short of being able to market several microcomputer games of potentially fabulous profitability, too. (One of my former partners and I have since started a new company to design such games.) About half of the $50K was back salary and accrued vacation time, and the rest was hard-earned dough I'd speculatively re-invested. I learned a lot they never teach you at Brown, including how to read a P&L statement, how to hire people and how to fire them, how to collect bills (and how to postpone paying bills), and especially how not to throw good money after bad. Let's see, $50,000 divided by seven years. . .well, it's cheaper than undergraduate education these days, but I guess the jury's still out on whether or not it was any sort of bargain."

Robin Chemers Illgen, New York City, has joined Goldman Sachs as an associate in the firm's investment banking division.

Dr. *Daniel J. Kalaskowski*, Baltimore, Md., has completed his specialty training in pediatric dentistry and is now on the staff at the Greater Baltimore Medical Center and the Community Pediatric Center of the University of Maryland Hospital, Baltimore.

Steve Lovas, Jr., Tigard, Oreg., is director of finance and administration for PACCOM, Inc., a division of Pacific Telecom, Inc., the sixth largest independent telephone company in the U.S. PACCOM is Pacific Telephone's non-regulated marketing division. His wife is *Judith Turner Lovas* '77.

Vincent V. McKnight and *Cynthia L. Garrett* were married in Washington, D.C., on Aug. 7. They are living in Takoma Park, Md. Cindy is a third-year student at Catholic University Law School, and Vincent is an associate at Ashcraft and Gerel.

Alexander Szabo II and his wife, Madeleine, of Rye, N.Y., report the birth of their second child, Tyler James, on Oct. 30. He joins his brother, Alexander Kyle III, who is 2.

Sarah E. Wald, Belmont, Mass., has been appointed assistant secretary of consumer affairs for the Commonwealth of Massachusetts in the administration of Governor Dukakis. Also, she has been elected president of the Women's Bar Association of Massachusetts.

Linda Stamm-Willig, Somerville, Mass., received her doctorate in clinical psychology from Rutgers in January. "My husband, John, and I are very excited. We bought a 100-year-old Victorian home on 142 Orchard St. and moved there in March. I've been working in the counseling center at Curry College in Milton, Mass., since September."

76 *Sandra Alpert*, Chicago, reports that she is "doing extremely well selling petrochemicals for Mobil Chemical Company in the Chicago area. I'm still footloose and fancy-free and welcome contact from any old friends in the area."

Lawrence S. Ames, Bolton, Mass., has been making wine at Nashoba Valley Winery in Concord since March 1981. "This year we led all other New England wineries in both the New England and Boston wine competitions. We won our first gold medal ever for our dry blueberry wine at the New England competition."

Michael L. Blumstein, New York City, is director, capital and teletext planning, for CBS Television. He is responsible for financial and business planning aspects of capital facilities and equipment in New York, Washington, and Los Angeles, as well as national teletext services being developed at CBS.

Bradley Brockmann, Ann Arbor, Mich., graduates this month from the University of Michigan Law School. He'll be an associate at the firm of Cleary, Gottlieb, Steen & Hamilton in New York City this fall. Last summer, he worked for Edwards & Angell in Providence and Willkie Farr & Gallagher in New York City. "Working as associates at Willkie Farr were *Jonathan Gottlieb* and *Genine Macks Fidler* '77. *Chris Graham*, *John Igoe* (with whom I roomed in Providence), and *Steve McInnis* are all E & A associates. It was great to see them, along with Dr. *Jessica Pep-*

itone, Dr. *Jane ("Baba") MacKenzie Dennison*, and *Scott Young*. I'm excited about moving to New York and thank God that law school is almost behind me. Thought I'd never make it."

Jeffrey Canin, Berkeley, Calif., is a securities analyst with Hambrecht and Quist in San Francisco. His address is 1671 Arch St., #5, Berkeley 94709.

Walter J. Drugan, Madison, Wis., is an assistant professor of engineering mechanics at the University of Wisconsin-Madison.

Timothy C. Forbes and *Anne Harrison* were married recently. They are living in New York City, where Tim is a film producer/director with Seven Seas Cinema, and Anne is a freelance book editor.

Eric S. Goldman, North Brunswick, N.J., writes that he has finally stopped moving from one state to the other and has returned to the neighborhood of his youth. "I now work with my family firm, Leonard Engineering, Inc., in Cranford, N.J." His home address is: 2 Petunia Dr., Apt. 1, North Brunswick 08902.

Alexandra Glowacki, Washington, D.C., is on leave from the Center for Strategic and International Studies at Georgetown University to work on a short-term foreign policy research study sponsored by the bipartisan American Political Foundation.

David Haettenschwiller, Berkeley, Calif., is assistant vice president in Wells Fargo's International Banking Group. "Am enjoying Northern California's beautiful outdoors to the fullest," he writes.

Robert Indech and his wife, Dr. *Christine Varney Indech*, of Melrose, Mass., report the birth of their daughter, Jennifer Lee, on Dec. 16. Robert is working as an engineer for the Department of Defense, and Chris is in her fourth year of orthopedic residency.

Gary D. Lawrence, New York City, is a vice president of Morgan Guaranty Trust Company of New York, "following the aerospace industry. I'm also directing a church choir in Manhattan," he writes.

Bob Mars and his wife, Jan, are living in Eden Prairie, Minn. Jan is assistant high school tennis coach, and Bob is manager of the Bloomington, Minn., branch of the W.P & R.S. Mars Company.

Nancy Padden has joined with Susan Werner O'Day (whose husband is *Mark O'Day* '77) and Loretta Cuda in the formation of Art Conservation Services, Inc., a studio established for the conservation and restoration of fine paintings. They are located at 30 Ipswich Street in Boston. "We welcome the opportunity to be of service to the Brown community."

Christopher P. Rauber married Kim P. Williams on May 8 in San Diego. *John Silbersack* '77 was an usher. Chris and Kim are living in San Francisco, where he is the editor of an industrial trade magazine for Miller Freeman Publications and she is a financial analyst for First Nationwide Savings.

Dr. *Debra Spicehandler* and her husband, Dr. Daniel Leonard, of New York City, report the birth of their son, Michael Scott Leonard, on March 14. Debra is completing her residency in internal medicine at New York University and will begin a fellowship in infectious diseases at NYU in July.

Bob Szostak and Mary Beth Bradigan, of Glenside, Pa., were married on Nov. 27. They are living in Wynnewood, Pa. Bob is an attorney for the Superior Court of Pennsylvania, and Mary Beth teaches at the Oak-lane Day School in Blue Bell.

Rebecca L. Wallin, San Francisco, is manager of staffing and staff development for the corporate banking group of Wells Fargo Bank in San Francisco. She completed her M.B.A. at Penn's Wharton School in 1981.

77

Wayne M. Barnstone has moved to the "suburbs" of Manhattan, Brooklyn Heights. *Anita Abraham Inz* and *Henry Asher* live one block away. "It's a lovely area—it reminds me of lower Thayer Street. I have left Irving Trust and am in the trade finance division of the First National Bank of Chicago's New York office. One of my responsibilities includes the solicitation of trade finance business with the People's Republic of China. So Chinese 4-5 has paid off."

Amy Finn Binder, New Rochelle, N.Y., is a public relations coordinator for the city of New Rochelle. She also reports the birth of her second son, Adam, who is nearly a year old. Ethan is almost 3.

Robert I. Feinberg, Newton Centre, Mass., graduated from the University of Pennsylvania Law School and is an associate with the Boston law firm of Parker, Coulter, Daley, and White, in its litigation department.

Janet E. Greenberg, Brookline, Mass., has become the assistant administrator for the department of medicine at Brigham and Women's Hospital in Boston.

Barbara Betts Howes, Newton Centre, Mass., is in her second year of law school at Boston College. She'll return to Providence this summer for a clerkship at Edwards and Angell.

Susan Newman Johanson and her husband, George, of Springfield, Vt., report the birth of their first child, James Arthur, on April 27. Last year, they attended the University of Massachusetts, where they did graduate work in education. "We would love hearing from anyone in our neck of the woods—Vermont and New Hampshire."

Benjamin R. Magee, Brooklyn, N.Y., is a freelance musician in New York City. His address is 238 President St., Brooklyn 11231.

Heather Magier and her husband, *Asher Rubinstein* (see GS), Plainview, N.Y., report the birth of their first child, Helen Betya Rubinstein, on Nov. 29. Heather is on leave from Columbia University Law School.

Robert S. Miller and his wife, Marci, of Arlington, Va., report the birth of their first child, Brian Seth Miller, on Aug. 30.

Amy L. Nathan, Washington, D.C., is a second-year student at the Georgetown University Law Center. Prior to this, Amy had spent four years as a newspaper reporter, two with the Gannett chain and two with the *Washington Post*.

Meryl D. Pearlstein, New York City, is a senior account executive at Ogilvy & Mather Advertising in New York.

Mary Wendell Rhea is a geologist for Texaco, U.S.A., in New Orleans.

Carolyn Rieder, Boston, is in her fourth year of graduate study at Harvard, where she is a Ph.D. candidate in psychology. She is working at McLean Hospital, where she is completing an internship in clinical psychol-

tainment law in the future," he writes.

Wynne Ennis Van Thoen, Lake Katonah, N.Y., writes: "I'll finish my M.A. in industrial psychology at New York University in December. In the meantime I'm working in an outpatient clinic called the New Rochelle Guidance Center, and, among other things, managing a restaurant called Eggs N' Such that is totally staffed by our patients."

Katherine D. Ventres is a first-year student at the J.L. Kellogg Graduate School of Management at Northwestern. "This is a grind after four years of fun work. I would love to have old friends come and visit and add some distractions. My address is 1249 Judson, Evanston 60202."

Denise Washington, Roosevelt, N.Y., has been selected as one of the Outstanding Young Women of America for 1982 by the Outstanding Young Women of America organization, Montgomery, Ala.

79

Tom Beckett and *Heidi J. Stamas* were married on June 19. They are living in New York City, where she is in her first year at Columbia Business School, and he is in his first year at New York University Law School. *Flora Del Presto*, *Andy Sommer* '78 and *Bill Bernstein* '78 were attendants at the wedding.

Richard M. Breslow, New York City, graduated from Georgetown University Law Center in May 1982 and passed the New York bar exam. He's an associate with the New York City law firm of Cravath, Swaine, & Moore.

Eric Chilton, New York City, is with Marine Midland Bank in the international department.

Julie A. Evans and *Ronald D. Frantz* are still living in Southern California and have moved into a condominium in Laguna Hills. Both are in sales, Ron with Burlington Industries and Julie with the Burroughs Corporation.

Beth Dyer Haskel and her husband, *Ethan*, of St. Louis, celebrated their second wedding anniversary on March 14. Beth is a legislative aide for the Home Builders Association of Greater St. Louis, and Ethan is in his fourth year of medical school at Washington University.

Laurie Friedman married Alon Harpaz on June 27. They are living in New Hyde Park, N.Y. Laurie is a researcher at the Stanley H. Kaplan Educational Center in Manhattan.

Louise A. Hohensee, Greenbelt, Md., is working as assistant editor at University Press of America in Washington, D.C. Friends can reach her at 5901 Cherrywood Ln., #201, Greenbelt 20770.

Colette A. Hyman, Minneapolis, Minn., is teaching women's studies at the University of Minnesota extension division. She has an M.A. in history.

Jed A. Kwartler, South Orange, N.J., graduates from New Jersey Medical School this month. He'll start his otolaryngology residence at University Hospital in Newark, N.J., in July. "I'm going on a sailing trip with medical school and Brown friends in June before starting my residency."

Dan Livingstone and *Debbie Pines* '80 were married in New York City on Feb. 26 and are living in Indianapolis.

Lauren A. McDonald and Howard A. Cole, Jr., were married on Sept. 11 in Pittsford, N.Y., and are living in Camden, N.J. *Dorothy McGill* was a bridesmaid. Lauren is a third-year medical student at Temple University School of Medicine, and Howard is employed by the U.S. Department of Labor.

Gil Neiger, Ithaca, N.Y., is a graduate student in computer science at Cornell University.

Patty Niemi, New York City, has been working in the fashion department at *Mademoiselle* magazine for more than two years.

John Rogers and his wife, *Susan Michael Rogers*, of New Lebanon, N.Y., report the birth of their first child, Catherine Meehan Rogers, on Dec. 22. The grandparents are *J. Graham Michael* and *Janice Peterson Michael* '50. Aunts are Dr. *Deborah Michael Lecky* '73 and *Linda Michael Thomas* '75.

Tommy L. Rueckert, Arlington, Va., is "still surviving the jaws of Reaganomics at the Department of Energy in Washington. I'm continuing to pursue a musical ministry singing and playing guitar. My album should be coming out in the fall, and in April I appeared at Big Mother Coffeehouse."

Nancie Spector, Cleveland, is a doctoral candidate at Case Western Reserve University and is completing her dissertation, "An Extensive Task Analysis of the Coding Subtest of the Wechsler Intelligence Scale for Children-Revised." She'll move to Providence in July to begin an internship in child clinical psychology at the Brown Clinical Psychology Internship Consortium.

Stacey Leigh Spector and *Richard W. Liedman* (see '78) were married on Aug. 28. They are living in New York City, where Stacey is a lawyer with Patterson, Belknap, Webb & Taylor.

Angela R. Stone, Dallas, is back from a year in the Virgin Islands and a year in Maui, Hawaii. "I'm working in a business partnership based in Dallas. We have a rapidly growing golf accessory business that has recently gone international. It's very satisfying being self-employed and moderately successful. I would love hearing from friends at my new address, 5813 Lovers Ln. #126B, Dallas 75225."

Lisa Moore Waranch and her husband, Terry, moved to Arlington, Mass., on March 1. She is working for the Millipore Corporation in Bedford, Mass. "I would love any old friends living in the Boston area or passing through to look us up at 39 Mary St., Arlington 02174. My business phone is (617) 275-9200."

80

Cynthia Cohn, Los Angeles, writes that after spending a year and a half studying acting and filmmaking and working in San Francisco, she is now a student in film production at USC, "exploring the landscape and the freeways of Los Angeles, making movies, writing screenplays, and getting my first taste of the reel world. Correspondence with the other world is desired. My address is 3910 Elderbank Dr., Los Angeles 90031."

C. Lynn Creviston, New York City, is at Columbia University, working on her master's degree in historic preservation.

Geoffrey C. Del Sesto, Boston, is a staff consultant for Computer Partners of Wellesley, Mass. "Being a consultant is fascinating. I help others solve their problems while constantly learning new applications. So far, I've helped design, code, test, and implement systems for Westinghouse and John Hancock Life Insurance. It would be great to hear from any fellow Zetes, trombonists, or other band members." He lives with *Michael Cohen* on Beacon Hill at 34 Myrtle St., #3, Boston 02114.

Alison L. Kane, Bronx, N.Y., is in her second year of Fordham University's Ph.D. program in clinical psychology. She co-authored a paper in September, entitled "A Different Drummer: Robert B. Carter and Nineteenth-Century Hysteria," which was published in the *Bulletin of the New York Academy of Medicine*.

Dale R. Karasek, Boston, has been working with the Emmanuel Gospel Center since he graduated. He's involved with Christian outreach to youth in the South End/Lower Roxbury neighborhoods of Boston.

Howard S. Klein, Baltimore, writes that he is "struggling through my last year of law school. Luckily, my responsibilities as legislative editor for the *University of Baltimore Law Review* fill otherwise drab days of legal lecture and part-time work for a small civil litigation firm. I resumed rowing this fall with the Baltimore Rowing Club and have been Vic Michaelson's disciple here (I do some coaching as well). I can't wait to stop living like a student so I can spend some (and make some?) money—for beers."

Steve James, Evanston, Ill., is graduating in June from the Kellogg Graduate School of Management at Northwestern University and plans to remain in Chicago to look for a job. *Ben Burnett* is also living there.

Bruce R. Jones has moved to the suburbs of Boston. "Toto, I don't think we're on the East Side anymore."

Mary Minow, Ann Arbor, received her master's degree in library science from the University of Michigan School of Library Science in December. She was given the Margaret Mann Award for outstanding professional promise and is working temporarily at the university, helping to organize an international conference for librarians from Latin America there this spring.

Thomas Waldron Philips, Tarrytown, N.Y., has been named director of the summer school at Hackley School in Tarrytown.

Debbie Pines and *Dan Livingstone* '79 were married recently in New York City and are living in Indianapolis.

Brad Richards, Iowa City, Ia., is finishing his second year of law school at the University of Iowa this month. He will be a summer associate with Squire, Sanders & Dempsey in Cleveland and welcomes any visits while he's there.

Susan D. Roseff, Albany, N.Y., is a medical student at Albany Medical College.

Julie D. Shapiro, Austin, Texas, is a second-year student at the University of Texas Law School. She will be working in Washington, D.C., this summer. Julie's address in Austin is 3517 North Hills Dr., #L-202, Austin 78731.

81

Betsy M. Allen, *Beth Connolly*, and *Debbie Pruzan* (see '82) are sharing a house in West Philadelphia. Betsy is a second-year student at the University of Pennsylvania School of Veterinary Medicine, and Beth is a second-year student at the Law School.

Laura Cutter is studying in Japan. "Please write, or come and visit," she writes. Her address is Kansai University, 333 Ogura, Hirakata-shi, Osaka, 573-Japan.

Lynn Green Gildiner and her husband, *Len Gildiner*, Philadelphia, report the birth of their daughter, Rachel Lauren, on Jan. 17, 1982. Lynn is on maternity leave from the post-baccalaureate pre-med program at the University of Pennsylvania.

Jayne M. Henderson, Newton, Mass., writes: "I'm currently surviving my first year at Boston College Law School after working for a year in the career development and placement office of the New England School of Law in Boston."

Judith Jones and *Richard Parker* were married in August in New York City. They are living in New Haven, Conn. *Ocie Irons* was the best man, and *Kurt Creamer* was one of the ushers. Judy is a second-year law student at Hofstra University, and Richard is a second-year medical student at Yale.

Frank J. Mello and *Claire Quillian* (see '82) were married on June 26 in Atlanta, Ga. They are living in Bolton, Conn. Frank's sister, *Jeanne Mello* '80, was a bridesmaid. The ushers included *Craig Mello*, *Chris Bryant*, and Brett Ferrari (all '82). The best man was *James F. Mello* '58, Frank's father. *Sally Cameron Mello* '58, Frank's mother, was in attendance. Frank is an engineer for Northeast Utilities.

Marybeth Paolino and Samuel Mather Andrews were married on March 19 in Providence, where they are living. Both are teaching at Moses Brown, Marybeth in mathematics and Samuel in science.

Barb Pendleton, Weston; Mass., has joined Computervision Corporation in Bedford, Mass., as a proposal specialist. She had worked for one year at Rhode Island Hospital Trust National Bank. Barb continues to sing in community groups and resides on a farm in Weston.

Julie Anne Reese is in Geneva, Switzerland, working for the United Nations in the International Telecommunications Union.

Katherine Swan Rutherford and *Andrew David Munts*, now both Munts-Rutherford, were married on Oct. 16 in Granville, Ohio. They are living in Dallas, but are moving to Amherst, Mass., this spring. The matron of honor was *Anne Rutherford Lindemann* and the best men were *Rob Campagna* '82 and *Mike Schield*.

Edward C. Shober, Jr., Williamsport, Pa., is a wire mill engineer in the wire rope division of the Bethlehem Steel Corporation.

Amy Voorhes, San Francisco, has joined Burson-Marsteller, a public relations/public affairs company, as an account executive. Previously, Amy had been an account executive with Lowry and Partners in San Francisco.

82

Steve Baer, Chicago, Ill., writes: "After a valiant but ill-fated campaigning stint for a West Virginia GOP senatorial candidate, I have settled in as director of education for Americans United for Life, a pro-life, public interest law firm."

Alison Berard and *Carolyn Bernstein* are sharing an apartment at 11 Linden Pl., Brookline, Mass. 02146. Alison is an assistant department manager at Filene's; Carrie

DEATHS

By Peter Mandel

Thomas Leo Keily '14, New Milford, Conn., owner of a paint manufacturing firm in Ossining, N.Y., for many years; Feb 21. Mr. Keily lived in Yonkers, N.Y., for most of his life. Phi Kappa. He is survived by his wife, Mary, c/o New Milford Nursing Home, 19 Poplar St., New Milford 06776. A brother was the late *John V. Keily* '11.

George Fremont Bliven '15, Charlestown, R.I., a senior partner in the Providence investment firm of Brown, Lisle, & Marshall before his retirement in 1973; March 20. Mr. Bliven was a paymaster in the U.S. Navy during World War I. Theta Delta Chi. Survivors include his wife, Evelyn, P.O. Box 142, Charlestown 02813; and three sons, *George, Jr.* '43, Edward, and *John* '45.

Emma L. Black '16, Providence, R.I.; March 16. Her brother was Dr. *Edward J. Black* '04. There are no immediate survivors.

William Black '20, New Rochelle, N.Y., founder and chairman of the Chock Full O' Nuts Corporation in New York City; March 7. Mr. Black graduated from the Columbia University School of Business in 1926. He then started a shelled nuts stand in the bottom of a Times Square office building that eventually grew into a chain of fast-food restaurants and a nationwide coffee business. He founded the Parkinson's Disease Foundation in 1957 and was a director of the New Rochelle Hospital. Survivors include his wife, Page, of Premium Point, New Rochelle 10801.

Woodworth Wright '21, Providence, R.I.; Oct. 5, 1982. He is survived by his sister, Francis Wright, Concord Ave., Cambridge, Mass. 02122.

Albert Otto Lundin '23, Wayzata, Minn., management consultant and publisher of a stock market trend guide; March 2. Before coming to Brown, Mr. Lundin attended the U.S. Naval Academy at Annapolis. He lived in New England after graduation, working as an engineer for several companies and becoming president of the Taunton Pearl Works in 1949. In 1951, he was offered the position of assistant secretary of the Navy, but turned it down for personal reasons. As an investment advisor, he was registered with the Securities and Exchange Commission and, after moving to Minnesota in 1964, he began publishing the *Lundin Market Trend Guide*. In his retirement years, he promoted and polished his simplified way of teaching piano playing to people who don't have the time or perseverance to struggle with scales and years of lessons. He copyrighted his four-page "Lundin Method for Playing the Piano Quickly." Delta Phi. Survivors include his son, *Robert A. Lundin* '53, BMTC P.O. Box 939, Al Khobar, Saudi Arabia; and a daughter, Eris Lundin Young.

Edythe Florence Reeves '23, '25 A.M., Middletown, R.I., dean of students at Cranston West High School prior to her retirement in 1964; Feb. 17. Miss Reeves began teaching Latin at Cranston High School in 1925, received a law degree from Northeastern in 1939, and returned to Cranston High in 1940 as head of the Latin department. She lived in Cranston for many years before moving to Middletown in the late 1950s. She is survived by her brother, Dr. *James A. Reeves* '36, 8 Kensington Rd., Cranston, R.I. 02905.

Hans Jordan Gottlieb '24, Upper Black Eddy, Pa., an English professor at New York University for many years; March 14. Mr. Gottlieb received an M.A. from Harvard in 1927 and a Ph.D. from NYU. in 1937. During World War II, he served in the U.S. Army Intelligence in Germany. In 1945, he returned to NYU as associate professor and remained there until his retirement. His poems appeared in a number of magazines and anthologies, including *Harper's* and *The New Yorker*. Survivors include his wife, Jerie, Box 43, Upper Black Eddy 18972; his daughter, Lucretia Gottlieb Floor, and granddaughter, *Victoria Floor* '76.

Dr. *Robert Mazet, Jr.* '24, Sun City, Ariz., former chief of orthopedic surgery at the Wadsworth Veterans Administration Hospital in Los Angeles and a retired rear admiral in the U.S. Navy Reserve; March 20. Dr. Mazet received his M.D. degree from Columbia in 1928 and went on to serve in the Navy as a surgeon. He was awarded the Bronze Star and the Navy Commendation Medal for his medical contributions during World War II. Following his return to reserve status in 1946, he assumed his position at the VA Hospital and, eventually, at UCLA as one of the original medical center faculty members. Dr. Mazet was a nationally recognized pioneer in the development of orthopedic prosthetic devices for crippled children. He was a diplomate of the American Board of Orthopedic Surgeons and a member of numerous professional organizations. He is survived by his wife, Catherine, 10602 Emerald Pt., Sun City 85351; sons Robert III and Bruce, and a brother, *Horace* '26.

Thomas Henry Stephens, Jr. '28, Dalton, Mass., owner and operator of the Stephens Insurance Agency in Dalton for forty-two years prior to his retirement in 1967; Feb. 20. Sigma Chi. Survivors include his wife, Barbara, 917 Main St., Dalton 01226; two daughters, Betty Pasenbach and Judith Klaubert; and a son, Gerald.

Brig. Gen. *Richard Henry Hopkins* '29, USA (Ret.), Morrisville, Pa., a distinguished veteran of World War II and a military aide to former Massachusetts Gov. Christian A. Herter; March 4. General Hopkins began his military career in the Falmouth National Guard Brigade in 1939. He served in the European Theatre and was awarded the Bronze Star for meritorious service in military operations in Belgium. He was promoted to brigadier general in 1956 and commanded the 104th AAA Brigade of the Massachusetts National Guard prior to his retirement in 1959. A resident of Pennsylvania since 1958, General Hopkins served for many years as a manager with the General Services Administration of the federal government. Delta Phi. Survivors include his wife, Constance, 1208 Linden Ave., Morrisville 19067; two sons, Richard, Jr., and Stephen; and a daughter, Margaret H. Freeman.

Ralph Bennett Milligan '29· Warren, R.I., a time clerk with Brown & Sharpe Manufacturing Company; March 16. He is survived by his wife, *Edith Oldham Milligan* '32· 42 Laurel Ln., Warren 02885.

Stephen Waterman, Jr. '29· North Danville, Vt., retired aviator and manager of the Burlington, Vt., and Bangor, Maine, airports; Aug. 26, 1982. Mr. Waterman trained to be a pilot with the Curtis Wright Corporation and went on to managerial positions with American Airlines and Boston and Maine Airlines. During World War II, he edited films for the War Department and served as a civilian instructor for Army, Navy, and Marine pilots. Survivors include his wife, Mabel Bernice, c/o Col. Edward W. Newell, Fort Devins, Mass. 01433. His father was *Stephen Waterman* 1886, and his brother was *Paul Waterman* '29·

Alton LeRoy Hambly, Jr. '37· Taunton, Mass., a self-employed real estate agent and long-time independent insurance agent; Feb. 16. Survivors include a brother, *Stafford H. Hambly* '30; and his son, Alton Hambly III, P.O. Box 381, Taunton 02870.

Edmond Joseph Schiller, Jr. '37· Barrington, R.I., manager of electrical engineers at the ITT Grinnell Corporation and former president of his own engineering consulting firm; March 19. Phi Sigma Kappa. He is survived by his wife, Esther, 10 Sherbrooke Rd., Barrington 02806.

Harm Edward Cook, Jr. '38· Wheaton, Ill., vice president of Tecology, Inc., in Columbus, Ohio, prior to his retirement; Aug. 25, 1982. Mr. Cook became an engineer with the Christopher Construction Company in Columbus before being named executive vice president and treasurer of that company. He lived in Michigan and Ohio for a number of years and in Puerto Rico, where he owned his own company. He is survived by a son, Michael Alden Cook, Fry Road, Katy, Texas 77449.

Henry Wright Stevenson, Jr. '38· Lincoln, R.I., executive director of the Providence Review Commission and former assistant state commissioner of education; March 30. Mr. Stevenson headed the Rhode Island Public Expenditure Council for a number of years, and then joined the Department of Education as the assistant commissioner for research and social aid issues. Upon retiring, he took the post on the Review Commission, which acts as the city's fiscal watchdog. He was treasurer of his class. Survivors include a daughter, Kim, and three sons, Johnathan, Frank, and Glen E. Stevenson, 189 Gladstone St., Cranston, R.I. 02920.

Edward Alanson Miller II '39 A.M., Kailua Oahu, Hawaii, a dispatcher for Aloha Airlines at Honolulu International Airport; Nov. 10, 1982. Mr. Miller received his B.A. from Oberlin College and, for several years, was an assistant professor in the French department at Brown. He is survived by his wife, Claudia, 1376 Kainui Dr., Kailua Oahu, Hawaii 96734.

Walter Neiman '46· Ardsley, N.Y., president of WQXR, the radio station of The New York Times Corporation; March 29. Mr. Neiman joined WQXR in 1953 as an executive assistant. He was named vice president for operations in 1965, and president of the station in 1974. Under his direction, WQXR began broadcasting on AM as well as FM, and transmitting its New York Philharmonic broadcasts nationwide. He was a director of the Associated Alumni and a former deputy mayor and village trustee of Ardsley. Survivors include his wife, Muriel, 41 Concord Rd., Ardsley 10502; and two sons, Peter and *Raymond* '84·

Robert Fairbanks Dover '55· Maitland, Fla., president of Slumber World, Inc., and owner of a Dairy Queen franchise in Orlando, Fla.; May 14, 1982. Mr. Dover was an operating manager and a buyer in furniture stores for a number of years. Delta Phi. Survivors include his wife, *Sara Harned Dover* '56· 2730 Saxon St., Allentown, Pa. 18103.

Robert Louis Girouard '71 Ph.D., Golden Valley, Minn., a former Brown administrator and an editor with the *Minneapolis Star* and *Cleveland Plain Dealer*; March 17. Mr. Girouard earned his B.A. from Tufts University in 1962 and a master's degree from Johns Hopkins University in 1963. After graduating from Brown, he stayed on as assistant director of admissions for two years. He then served as editor of the *Mankato Free Press* in Minnesota and, for three years, as editorial page editor of the *Minneapolis Star*. Last fall, he became chief editorial writer for the *Cleveland Plain Dealer*. He was a member of the *BAM's* National Advisory Board. Survivors include his wife, Nancy, 4215 Beverly Ave., Golden Valley 55422, and two sons. The family was moving from Minnesota to Cleveland at the time of Mr. Girouard's sudden death.

Julian H. Gibbs, Amherst, Mass., president of Amherst College since 1979 and professor of chemistry at Brown from 1959 to 1979; Feb. 20, following a heart attack suffered the previous day while skiing. The 1946 Amherst graduate received his master's degree and his Ph.D. in 1950, both from Princeton. He studied at Cambridge on a Fulbright Scholarship, worked eight years in industry, and then joined the Brown faculty. While at Brown, he received a Guggenheim Fellowship and a second Fulbright, both in 1967, and was named a NATO Fellow in 1975. He also served as chairman of the Faculty Policy Group and headed the search committee that recommended the selection of Donald F. Hornig as Brown's president in 1970. Brown awarded him an honorary doctor of laws degree in 1981. The

BROWN ALUMNI MONTHLY
Brown University Box 1854
Providence, Rhode Island 02912

ADDRESS CORRECTION REQUESTED

Non-Profit Org.
U.S. POSTAGE
PAID
Permit No. 19
Burlington, VT 05401

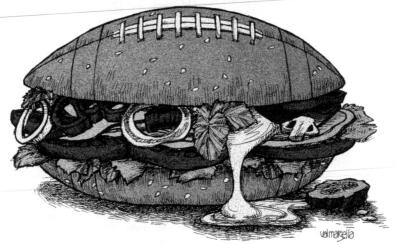

BROWN ALUMNI MONTHLY
Brown University Box 1854
Providence, Rhode Island 02912

ADDRESS CORRECTION REQUESTED

Non-Profit Org.
U.S. POSTAGE
PAID
Permit No. 19
Burlington, VT 05401